Critical Appr...
Cr...

What is creative writing? In ...ical *Approaches to Creative Writing*, Graeme Harper draws on both creative and critical knowledge to look at what creative writing is, and how it can be better understood. Harper explores how to critically consider creative writing in progress, while also tutoring the reader on how to improve their own final results. Throughout the book, Harper explains the nature of 'creative exposition', where creative writing is closely and directly examined in practice as well as through its final results. This book aims to empower you to develop your own critical approaches so that you can consider any creative writing situations you face, develop creative exposition that can be applied to writing problems, provide you with more creative choices and assist you in building your creative writing strengths.

Graeme Harper is Professor of Creative Writing and Dean at Oakland University, Michigan, USA. For over a dozen years, he assessed creative writing for Britain's Arts and Humanities Research Council. Awarded the first doctorate in Creative Writing in Australia, he holds a second doctorate in Creative and Critical Writing from the University of East Anglia, UK. An award-winning fiction writer, he examines creative writing in universities throughout the world and is editor of the journal *New Writing* (Taylor & Francis).

GRAEME HARPER

Critical Approaches to Creative Writing
Creative Exposition

Routledge
Taylor & Francis Group
NEW YORK AND LONDON

First published 2019
by Routledge
2 Park Square, Milton Park, Abingdon, Oxon OX14 4RN

and by Routledge
711 Third Avenue, New York, NY 10017

Routledge is an imprint of the Taylor & Francis Group, an informa business

© 2019 Graeme Harper

British Library Cataloguing-in-Publication Data
A catalogue record for this book is available from the British Library

Library of Congress Cataloging-in-Publication Data
A catalogue record has been requested for this book

ISBN: 978-1-138-93154-1 (hbk)
ISBN: 978-1-138-93155-8 (pbk)
ISBN: 978-1-315-67971-6 (ebk)

Typeset in Joanna MT and Din
by Deanta Global Publishing Services, Chennai, India

For those who seek to know more

Contents

Acknowledgments

Critical Approaches to Creative Writing owes its origins and its outlook to many people and bountiful influences. It is impossible to acknowledge here everyone who deserves acknowledgment. I therefore offer my sincerest thanks and my abashed apologies! Just some of those to whom I owe a debt of gratitude include Professor Jon Cook, Director of the Centre for Creative and Performing Arts at the University of East Anglia (UEA), who mentored my doctoral work there. Sir Malcolm Bradbury, for his frequent kindness and heartfelt observations. Thanks to Professor Vic Sage and Dr Clive Sinclair, who examined my second finished doctoral submission and, in a space of a few hours examination, encouraged me thereafter to delve more deeply into ways we can explore creative writing practice. Prior to those UEA days, thanks to Professor Stephen Muecke, most recently at the University of Adelaide, who mentored my first doctoral journey at the University of Technology, Sydney (UTS). Thanks to Brian Matthews and Rosemary Sorensen who examined the results of that first journey – and produced a report combining kindness and erudition that has stood as my aspirational model for examining creative writing over many institutional appointments and my consideration of creative writing masters and doctoral submissions from around the globe, now numbering many dozen. Earlier still, my thanks to Professor Chris Lloyd, of the University of New England. Chris opened my mind to the idea that human practices and critical understandings have layered and intersecting elements, and that to approach them accurately we require similar methods and comparable knowledge. Thanks to the Peer Review Board of *New Writing: The International Journal for the Practice and Theory of Creative Writing* (Taylor & Francis). The wonderful work submitted to *New Writing*, and reviewers' responses to that work, regularly informs my thoughts. The Peer Review Board is itself indicative of the variety of points of view and life stories we see when we talk about 'creative writers' as a group and creative writing as a widely loved human endeavor. For example, Peer Review Board member Sir Andrew Motion, ever generous as he has always been, Dianne Donnelly, Bronwyn Williams, Jeri Kroll, notable artistic director Liam Browne, who is also an excellent novelist – in fact, the entire *New Writing* Peer Review Board, its long established members and new members alike. Thanks also to colleagues on assessment panels and senior assessment panels at Britain's Arts and Humanities Research Council (AHRC), to which I was appointed between 2003 and 2015, assessing creative and critical writing applications. Similarly, thanks to fellow appointees on the EU Commission's DGX Directorate 'Panel of Experts' and to those at the Hong Kong Research Council, where I have seen many exciting projects proposed. Thanks to the dozens of creative writers and creative writing students who have attended live-streamed events of the International Center for Creative Writing Research (ICCWR), now in its 20th year. And to the many friends and colleagues who have presented their work at the Great Writing International Creative Writing Conference, which I have directed now for over 21 years (again at Imperial College, London, in 2018). Warm thanks to my students, particularly those masters and doctoral students whose projects and approaches have been a frequent source of inspiration. Thanks to Zoë Meyer at Routledge, for all her encouragement and support. And thanks to Polly Dodson, who contracted this book. Thanks greatly, Polly, for setting this book in motion, for the thoughts that assisted in forming it, and for ensuring the work could reach fruition. Finally, thanks to Myles and Tyler, two fabulous sons, and to my wife Louise, with all my love always.

The history of this book is modestly both public and personal. Having completed the first doctorate in Creative Writing awarded in Australia (Boyd, 2009), a fact of which I was then unaware, I was still seeking more knowledge about what it was I was doing as a creative writer, so I signed up for a PhD in Creative and Critical Writing at Britain's University of East Anglia (UEA). Creative writing at UEA was internationally renowned.

The fact was, the more I understood (or at least perceived that I understood) some of what we might call the 'technical' aspects of creative writing (in my case, particularly fiction writing) the more I wanted to understand what creative writing was as a practice, generally, and how that practice produced results of many kinds. I also wanted to understand the relationship, if there was a relationship, between what I was discovering on a personal level about the actions and results of *doing* creative writing and what might be a general understanding of creative writing and the actions involved in it. That pursuit of knowledge about creative writing, from the point of view of being a creative writer, was likewise what ultimately drew me to the USA, where I have now lived for some years, and where this book is being written.

The focus on the 'doing' of creative writing has always been paramount for me, as the approach in this book exemplifies.

Like many other undergraduates, I had formally studied novels, poetry, plays as a reader or audience for these things. However, that study did not seem to equip me sufficiently for what I was experiencing when I first began to write creatively (fiction in particular, but also scripts and the occasional poem). I was still feeling that way when, after winning a national award for fiction writing (by inference because I allegedly knew something about creative writing), I was accepted into the University of Technology, Sydney (UTS) to study for what was ultimately to be that first completed doctorate in Creative Writing in Australia.

Given the status of a doctorate as the highest level of academic degree, a degree that also carries with it the notion of qualifying a person to teach at university level, this should have meant some confidence in what I was doing. However, I really did not have the apparatus, the methodology or even the language to describe what I was doing, and certainly not to describe it to the extent I felt I should have been able to describe it as a doctoral student in the field. There was no satisfactory established means of analyzing what I was doing, thinking and experiencing as a fiction writer, from the point of view of *being* a creative writer and of *doing* creative writing. Frankly, something seemed amiss.

In one sense, I was setting out on an exhilarating adventure, in another sense I was alarmingly adrift. Biographical evidence suggests plenty of creative writers have felt adrift while trying to compose their works. That in itself was not the salient point. The difference was that in my instance I was undertaking an advanced degree at a university and simply saying 'sorry, I don't have the tools, the approach or the language to do this' was not an option.

The basic problem was palpable, and it is the problem that this book recognizes and seeks to dissect. While we have long critically explored works of creative writing, the biographical details concerning authors of those works, the cultural contexts of those works and even dissected the linguistic or semantic elements of the creatively written text, we have not deeply considered creative writing as a practice, in terms of the knowledge and understanding involved in the practice, and as this relates to its many outcomes. Not truly. There is certainly a range of anecdotal evidence. Individual creative writers over a considerable amount of time have offered their comments and thoughts on their experiences. Sometimes emotional, incredibly personal thoughts have been expressed; sometimes erudite, skillful observations have been made. These are widely available, along with external critical analyses by those who are focused mostly on the final results of creative writers' practice. Additionally, there are many explorations of the teaching of creative writing. Occasionally these pedagogic discussions have been offered up as explorations of creative writing when in fact they are really about the teaching of creative writing. The differentiation between the field itself and its teaching seems not always well-discerned; while equally at times pedagogic research has assisted in unearthing new ideas about creative writing, so suggesting a separation between subject research and pedagogic research is almost certain to be unproductive. Palpably, however, what remains absent is a concerted critical discourse for creative writing and creative writers.

This book seeks to address that absence, delving into the underlying practices of creative writing, and offering examples of the apparatus and the methodologies, and the basics of a language, for creative writers to explore critically, consider and perhaps even advance our understanding of creative writing. The absence of these things has been a defining factor for far too long. It was how things were as I began my period of Doctor of Creative Arts (DCA) study at UTS in Australia and, even though that period of writing and study was extremely positive and led to further personal understanding, it remained the case when I arrived in England to begin my PhD in Creative and Critical Writing at UEA. Despite increased global interest in critical approaches to creative writing, I would be more hopeful than truthful if I said that the absence had been addressed by the time I arrived here in the USA some seven years ago.

Critical Approaches to Creative Writing is the result of work undertaken in the USA, the United Kingdom and Australia, and informed further by excursions and adventures beyond. It emerges from the central thought that creative writers are distinctive and that we think and act in distinctive ways, in and through our practice of creative writing, in whatever genre we might be working. This has led to many secondary thoughts. For example, it might have been at that moment of my arrival at the University of East Anglia, while visiting an archetypal cluttered little bookstore near Norwich's 15th century Guildhall, that I rekindled my questioning of why throughout time all great critics of literature had not all also been great novelists or great poets or great short story writers or great playwrights. This renewed wondering was not by way of snide assertion! It was not to suggest that all critics of literary works secretly wanted to be creative writers. Rather, with the concrete ziggurats of the University of East Anglia down the road, representing the learning of creative writing and the contemporary world, used books stacked pell-mell all around me, and the ancient Norwich Castle and Norwich Cathedral both also in sight, it struck me I might also be close to a discoverable truth. Quite simply, that for creative writers there *are* distinctive ways of thinking, as well as ways of responding to the world, and ways of interpreting facts, and ways of moving between the intellect and the imagination, often fluidly, seamlessly – and that individual and general manifestations of these ways are, in fact, discoverable.

Not everything in this book works from a knowledge base dominated, as often is the case in creative writing programmes, by the critical study of literature. If there is something creative writers often do it is draw eclectically on types and domains of knowledge. We do this in seeking out both content and subject knowledge and in determining literal and metaphoric ways of understanding such things as structure, pace, voice, point of view, even beauty and psychological and physiological appeal. Personally, before venturing into doctoral work in creative writing, I completed a master's degree concentrating on historiography, involving a varied range of reading in the philosophy of history. I find myself returning to this early training when considering how I select and order my critical thinking.

What philosophies of history tell us is that history can be written in many fashions. For the creative writer such an idea is hardly remarkable. Part of the joy of creative writing is knowing that there are creative choices available to us and that the application of those choices is something we each can enjoy exploring, imaginatively and intellectually. Creative writing is imaginative inquiry, not always determinate, inventively questioning. The writing of history is, by and large, a measured combination of found facts and historian's interpretations that lead to premises and aim to suggest truthful historiographical conclusions. Skilled historiographers say we should endcavor to balance between these two aspects, facts and interpretations if we are to write history accurately, create those valid arguments, those well-reasoned premises, and reach valid conclusions. For an historian to err on the side of merely accumulating facts results in what renowned historiographer E. H. Carr once said was akin 'antiquarianism' (Carr, 1961: 7). Antiquarianism is only accumulating rather than the assessing of relevance and significance. To err on the opposite side, that is to overemphasize interpretation, is a different kind of 'heresy', as Carr would call it. In that case, the error belies the potential for truth, creating a kind of interpretative anarchy that does not take into account our common-sense existence, whereby we humans are able to communicate with each other and to exist together in relatively organized and agreed ways.

Fact, interpretation, relevance, significance, argument, premise, conclusion, maintaining balance: these certainly seemed to me productive concepts to underpin the writing of this book, and ones with which support the conclusions about critical approaches to creative writing ultimately presented here.

Any creative writer recognizes that one or other final work we might release to a reader or audience — if ever there is a final work we release to a reader or audience, not all creative writing produces a final work — this final work is far from the only that has been or is going on when we are writing. In fact, it is only one component of what we do. In being so, it can be considered both a very significant thing and the least significant thing about what we do. That is because primarily we creative writers are engaged in the practice of creative writing, the doing of it. That is the simple, determining, universal observation. Thus the major premise behind this book: that creative writers are creative writers because we are (or in some cases because we have been) engaged in the practice of creative writing. All thinking here follows from this.

As creative writers, we produce evidence of our practice (some of this is material evidence, some of it is indeed personal evidence, incorporating our sensory perceptions and our experiences, some of it is inferred or circumstantial evidence). The critical apparatus available to us to explore and interpret what we do is considerable, given that we draw widely on direct observations and the observations on others, on established human knowledge and on our imaginations. We also use analogy and analogical reasoning to create relationships between our personal understanding and that of readers or audiences, or to speculate on why things are, or how things might be. All of this is highly significant to our exploration of the truths of what we do as creative writers and how we do it. Creative writing is both an individual practice, based in the self (you, me, other creative writers), and a holistic one, reflective of cultural, societal and historical influences upon us and upon those around us.

Critical Approaches to Creative Writing owes its character to many influences, personal and public, national and international, discoveries through creative writing practice and through examining the practices and outcomes released to the world by others. Here in the USA, more than a quarter of a century after my first visit, longer since my first exploration of work published here about creative writing, the influence of composition studies is notable. The role of the workshop as a well-established site of creative writing education in the USA is prominent. My publishing of works of fiction with a publisher here cannot but ground something of my thinking.

Most recently, I have been one of the founding members of the US Creative Writing Studies Organization (CWSO).

Is *Critical Approaches to Creative Writing* a work of creative writing studies? Defensibly so, given how it is situated in the concerted critical study of creative writing. The following, as of December 2017, is the description of 'What is Creative Writing Studies?' on the CWSO website. This statement might evolve in the years ahead, but it encapsulates the organizational position as it stands at this time:

> Creative writing studies is an emerging discipline that is currently in the process of defining itself. In his 2009 *College English* article "One Simple Word: From Creative Writing to Creative Writing Studies," Tim Mayers describes creative writing studies as a field of scholarly inquiry and research that he divides into three overlapping strands: pedagogical, historical, and advocacy-oriented. In her 2011 book *Establishing Creative Writing Studies as an Academic Discipline*, Dianne Donnelly defines the field as the exploration of "the history of creative writing, its workshop model as its primary practice, and the discipline's major pedagogical practices." Both acknowledge that this field is still young and will need further research and investigation before it can become its own discrete discipline.
>
> (Creative Writing Studies Organization)

The dynamics of organizational influence make for an interesting background discussion to this book. Organizations focusing on creative writing tend to offer a conference, a journal or magazine, and to have an online presence. They promote the positive professional impact of your organizational membership enabling you to engage fully with each of these things. While based in Britain, I became inaugural Chair of the Higher Education Committee (2008–2011) at the National Association of Writers in Education (NAWE). That experience alone is often a personal reminder of the role organizations can, and have played in contributing to how we talk about creative writing, how we formalize those discussions and what influence those discussions can have.

In addition to the newly emerged CWSO, the USA is also home to the influential Association of Writers and Writing Programs (AWP). Influential not least because of its large-scale (it currently includes 'nearly 50,000 writers' and '550 college and university creative writing programs', substantially from the USA), the AWP notes its mission as 'to foster literary achievement, advance the art of writing as essential to a good education, and serve the makers, teachers, students, and readers of contemporary writing' (Association of Writers and Writing Programs). Here too the Conference on College Composition and Communication (CCCC), an organization within the National Council of Teachers of English (NCTE), founded in 1949 (18 years before the AWP), holds an annual convention that embraces creative writing among the many forms of writing it explores from both a teaching and research point of view. The CCCC describes itself as 'the world's largest professional organization for researching and teaching composition, from writing to new media' (Conference on College Composition and Communication).

All of these organizations in some way influence the work in this book – by their declarations of what they do, whom they do it for and why they do it in the first place, and how engaging with that has impacted on my critical thinking. More specifically, and finally, *Critical Approaches to Creative Writing* emerges from my personal history over three continents. In Australia, I started my creative writing and I published my first work. My period of doctoral research there was brought into being by two professors with backgrounds in semiotics. From memory, I am not sure I entirely understood at the time what semiotics entailed! I was mentored during that doctorate primarily by one of those professors, an ethnographer, a literary and cultural theorist, a creative writer, with an additional background in linguistics and a strong interest in indigenous cultures. A good deal of this was influential. The library at the University of Technology, Sydney, was an inner city one (UTS having only recently become a university, evolving from the former New South Wales Institute of Technology, which had also only recently incorporated The School of Design of the former Sydney College of the Arts). That library's holdings were thus an eclectic mix of theoretical and practical works, across the professions, in industrial disciplines, in the arts, designed for students with diverse backgrounds and career trajectories. That diverse mix of reading, aimed at a range of people with a range of life goals and life stories, had an influence that is still evident in my thinking behind this book and my approach to it.

Almost at the end of my time in Australia, I was in the library of the University of New England (UNE) in Armidale on the Northern Tablelands of New South Wales. Armidale is a city of just over 23,000. Surrounded by large farms focused on beef cattle and sheep, it was a contrast to the inner city Sydney life hugging the main UTS campus. Idly considering what to do next after my Doctor of Creative Arts degree, I was upstairs in the UNE library in a collection devoted to further study opportunities when I came across a catalogue for Britain's University of East Anglia (UEA). I first noticed a photograph of the novelist, John Fowles, whose novel *The Collector* I had read and thought both frightening and astonishing. Fowles had been a visiting writer at UEA. On the next page, or thereabouts, was a picture of Malcolm Bradbury (later Sir Malcolm), who founded the Masters in Creative Writing at UEA. Pictured with him was one of the first graduates of that programme, Kazuo Ishiguro (who would go on to be awarded the 2017 Nobel Prize for Literature). The description of the PhD in Creative and Critical Writing at UEA was evocative, not least supported by those photos. My supervisor had research interests in Romantic and post-Romantic literature and culture, and a strong interest in philosophy. Erudite and widely respected, he was the director of the university's Centre for Creative and Performing Arts. The UEA library was well-stocked with contemporary writing, fiction in particular, works by authors I had not previously encountered, as well varied works of European philosophy, reflective of what was then both a strong philosophy programme and a strong concentration in modern European languages. This together with volumes reflecting the university's internationally significant work in the field of linguistics. The American Studies program at UEA was prominent, and many of the contemporary works of fiction I was soon discovering in the library were American. As it happens Malcolm Bradbury, who many associate solely with the late 20th century boom in creative writing education in Britain, was formally a professor of American Studies. The annual UEA Literary Festival had begun two years before my arrival. Entirely unprepared for this, I was soon exposed to live readings by creative writers as well-known as Robert Coover, Salman Rushdie, Arthur Miller, Ian McEwan, Mario Vargas Llosa, David Lodge, Toni Morrison, Graham Swift, T.C. Boyle, Doris Lessing and so many more. Sometimes meeting them after their readings. Creatively and critically all this was a long way from where I had been. As it turned out, it was a step to where I was going. Invited along with the Masters in Creative Writing students to the annual gatherings that Malcolm and Elizabeth Bradbury held in their well-known Heigham Grove home, I also experienced my first sense of connected personal histories, connected beliefs perhaps, certainly connected predilections.

Thinking of creative writers as members of a community of practice, a community with shared creative and critical interests, has its origins in those convivial Bradbury evenings. That sense of common endeavor heartily informs this book. I owe that informing to Malcolm and Elizabeth, and I owe a sense of the importance of it to the way in which Malcolm encouraged and supported it.

This book would not otherwise have emerged if not that, after my periods of study, I began a full-time university teaching life. In that life I have regularly examined creative writing programmes, a great many of them now, as well as assessed higher degree work in creative and critical writing from around the world. I have now undertaken doctoral and masters assessments of this kind, globally, for over 20 years. Today I consider between two and ten doctoral submissions in creative and critical writing each year. Every one of these enlightens me in some way, and that ongoing engagement with creative writers exploring their practices and their critical understandings is a joy and a strong influence too on *Critical Approaches to Creative Writing* – both the great submissions I have read and the not so great submissions.

For over a dozen years from the early 2000s, I was an appointed panelist and later senior panelist at the United Kingdom's Arts and Humanities Research Council (AHRC), primarily assessing applications for funding for creative and critical writing, from those submitted by advanced degree students to those submitted by my academic peers. Saying 'yes' or saying 'no' to funding someone's project certainly concentrates the mind. During my time at the AHRC, this regularly returned me to questions of facts and interpretation. Around the time I began at the AHRC, I also spent three years as a member European Commission's 'Panel of Experts' on a program in its Education and Culture Directorate, where multi-arts projects competed for funding. Creative writing barely dented the Commission's budget, compared to applications for projects in the visual and performing arts, in film and television and most particularly in new, digital media.

The importance of being able to articulate what we creative writers do, how we can critically discuss it and what ultimately are its outcomes, was never more obvious to me than it was when I sat on that panel. Interestingly, so many of the funded projects in the other arts were heavily dependent on the input of creative writers doing good creative writing! Finally, in 2004 I was involved with colleagues in the the launch and subsequently I have been involved in the editing of *New Writing: The International Journal for the Practice and Theory of Creative Writing* (Taylor & Francis), regularly publishing new work in creative and critical writing from around the world. *New Writing*'s many authors, and its dedicated editorial board and peer reviewers, have fundamentally informed the writing of this book.

Those influences have brought about *Critical Approaches to Creative Writing*; together, that is, with my own creative writing practice and my regular consideration of it. I cannot replicate any of these influences exactly for the reader, of course: they are personal, as much of what we do in creative writing is personal. They might or might not have many or a few familiar elements for you. Each reader will bring to this book their own experiences, thoughts and feelings. There is, however, a suggestion here, a strong sense, a studied critical judgement that there is a community of practice we creative writers occupy. There is a commitment further to acknowledging that our creative writing community, whatever genre we are working in, or stage of creative writing life we are at, or place and time we occupy, produces evidence of our creative writing practice. That we can explore, individually and together, interpretations of that practice, construct arguments about it, offer premises, come to conclusions. There is a belief too that all this will better inform us about our own creative writing as well as assist us in better understanding the practices of other creative writers.

Rochester Hills
Michigan, USA
June 2018

REFERENCES

Association of Writers and Writing Programs (2018) *Overview.* www.awpwriter.org/about/overview (accessed December 28, 2017).

Boyd, N. (2009) Describing the creative writing thesis: A census of creative writing doctorates, 1993–2008. *TEXT: Journal of Writing and Writing Courses*, 13 (1), April. www.textjournal.com.au/april09/boyd.htm (accessed December 26, 2017).

Carr, E.H. (1961) *What Is History?* New York: Knopf.

Conference on College Composition and Communication (1998–2018) *Home.* http://cccc.ncte.org/cccc (accessed December 27, 2017).

Creative Writing Studies Organization (n. d.) *Home.* www.creativewritingstudies.com/ (accessed December 27, 2017).

WHAT IS CREATIVE WRITING?

Because creative writing has been given a specific name it must therefore be recognizable to us in some way? This is a question widely posed in education and in literary criticism. It is also a question regularly explored in pop culture. In that vein, we can think of the stock characters of the quirky poet, the impoverished novelist, the media savvy screenwriter. The more formal answer to the question usually involves someone pointing to synonyms for creativity, words such as invention, novelty, originality, innovation, vision, and making these the defining strokes with which to paint their picture of the practice of creative writing. In this way, we end up with the wonderfully redundant suggestion that creative writing is recognizable because it is writing that is creative.

Standing proudly in front of this tautological silliness, perhaps shuffling uncomfortably for effect, those answering the question then most often turn to works of creative writing. Perhaps a bright poem, a complex novel, a thoroughly thumbed loose-leaf copy of a screenplay, identify characteristics, perhaps with a quote or two of the finest and feistiest passages, a laudatory 'See!' and a cheery chuckle. This is of course akin to pointing doggedly at a mid-summer vegetable garden, with its clustered green beans and tomatoes now red on the ground, in order to explain how the vegetables were grown.

Were these responses due to an inherent human laziness or our lack of ability to critically engage with our many other writing practices they might be more palatable. But it seems that it mostly comes about because we have yet to fully ask the question, to then explore it concertedly, and in doing so to approach an informed discussion of what creative writing might be. There is additionally a floating romantic notion – small wooden rowboat, languid green lake, colorful petals scattered in the water all about, that kind of thing – that if we disturb creative writing by daring to query it, if we tap the quirky creative writer on her or his curiously bony shoulder and ask what on earth they are doing, a terrible oozing darkness will immediately descend upon us, and all will be lost.

Of course, it could my turn here is unduly melodramatic, and that in fact the real reason we have not been more attentive to the question of nomenclature, for a start, is that creative writing is so well-named that there really is no other word for it. That there is no other appellation that can reach the real character of creative writing, and any attempt to find one is doomed to failure. Therefore, unlike the domestic dog, whose characteristics defining it as a dog are maybe clear enough, even if the word 'dog' does little at all to assist that definition, and the word 'automobile', which goes a definitional step further, even if the description does nothing to tell us how to drive one, the term 'creative writing', much like the alarming exclamation 'Bang!' and your cat's empathetic onomatopoeic 'meow' says all it needs to say to succinctly tell us all we need to know.

And yet, we clearly do not know all we need to know about creative writing as a personal practice and as a practice embraced in cultures and across cultures. If we did, there would be recognized paradigms concerning our thoughts and our actions, comprehensive methodological outlines, developed theories about creative writing practices, which might periodically be challenged but that are articulated and that exist nevertheless. There would be epistemological investigations (that is, regular and advanced discussions of what knowledge types, forms and conditions creative writing contains), and ontological positions (for example, how does any one action of creative writing, your creative writing actions, mine, anybody's, relate to our perceived reality or realities?). I am not saying baldly here in this Introduction that these things *should* all unequivocally exist for the practice of creative writing (investigating if and how they could is a key reason for this book!), only that they *would* exist, in some more developed form than they currently do exist. After all, they do exist in many other fields of human endeavor.

Even the things we know at present about creative writing as a human practice stop short of explaining the practice in a way that conjoins its individualist characteristics – the things one creative writer does and thinks, and why they do and think these ways – with exchangeable knowledge between fellow humans, even if that knowledge is some ways incomplete. Knowledge, that is, about the choices made and the results of each of these choices, on both an individual and a shared human level. Compare this with what we know and discuss about human practices as random, varied and wide-ranging as different sports, musical performance, chemistry, mechanical engineering, organizational management, psychology, film-making, sociology or physical therapy, and the absence of a more concerted critical discussion of creative writing practice, in practice, and of that practice, is astonishing.

If you doubt any of this – and you rightly might, the case has not yet been made here, after all! – ask yourself why any creative writing workshop (the world's most common venue for creative writing education), one you might have been in, at any time at all, relied almost entirely on the encouragement of opinion about students' work-in-progress or on completed pieces of work by students or others?

Alternatively, how much of that workshop time was used to consider individual and group perceptions of a particular compositional practice or, taking evidence of shared practices across the group, how much of it involved comparisons and contrasts between individual understandings of what these practices might mean? For example, did you discuss what constituted for one creative writer or another in the workshop the concept of a beginning, an opening, a start, and how those personal concepts manifested themselves in a particular creative writing practice and from that practice or, more accurately, set of practices, in a set of results – say in the writing of a poem or in the writing of a short story? Not, that is, only how the physical forms looked, but how your thinking and your feeling and your understanding actually functioned, how it was formed, how it influenced your actions, and how it became manifest in your practice and that practice produced results? To continue the example, did you have a discussion of where each workshop participant felt creative writing began? Is it at the first word typed on a page or screen? Several months or weeks earlier at the first sign of an idea for a piece of creative writing? In another creative writing practice at another time – putting a new project on hold until you finished the previous one? If you didn't discuss where creative writing began for you, what prompt did your workshop professor use to ask you to begin? If you didn't have a discussion of your thinking and feeling before you began the workshop how was it possible for what you did during the workshop to be judged?

On a connected front, how much of the workshop considered ideals of satisfaction – given that creative writing is both a personal and a cultural practice, with a role in self-expression, a role in many creative industries (in industries associated with publishing, media, theatre, music, leisure software, for example), a role in supporting other educational goals (language learning, encouraging creativity)? Did you begin, perhaps, with a discussion of a range of writerly accomplishments and an agreement of how some of these might be met in your case, or were the accomplishments set out more in the manner of particular literary outcomes or demonstration of particular stylistic, structural or genre conventions or approaches, for example? Were you offered alternative viewpoints on satisfaction or was there one primary viewpoint, or a very small number of viewpoints, most likely focused on an end material result of your creative writing, which formed the primarily element of your assessment during the workshop?

This small selection of questions is simply a starting point, and they are related to one instance of creative writing happening in our world (in this case one in education, and a particular one: the creative writing workshop). If we are seeking to look for creative writing's distinctiveness, in order to explore how we each might better come to critically define and investigate it, and in doing so to further understand it, we don't necessarily need to focus on its educational identity. We could simply think of how it manifests itself in one human life or another or another.

You might have thought a particular acquaintance would make a great character in a short story and so you began to write that story. You might, or most likely might not, have revealed this plan to your acquaintance. Perhaps you responded to something by writing some poetry, a poignant couplet, a dramatic monologue, some wildly impulsive free verse (no indictment of free verse, incidentally! 'After the snow falls / after the quiet deer', that kind of thing). Being both the application of feeling and the application of personal analysis, creative writing is frequently a response to something or to someone. You might have decided to actually script the family recording that you are planning to send to those long-suffering grandparents, at least a little to add some structure this time, and now find yourself encouraging your family to take on fictional roles, ham it up a little. Still you wonder why your grandparents looked a little pained when each year they tell you they love getting your holiday videos. Creative writing is so often borne on personal perception, on empathy or attempts at empathy, as much as it is on familiar public communication.

Form, style, type, genre, while these indeed are recognizable components of recognizable results of creative writing, the practices that shape these are not bound up in the event of creative writing but come from our post-event understanding of how these aspects manifest themselves in end results. You can be writing creatively without necessarily having begun at the point of formal or stylistic or genre definition. Creative writing can be spontaneous and casually responsive, even occasionally fortuitous, or it can be planned and organized and created to a predetermined purpose. Of course, we also encounter the great many results of creative writing in so many of our leisure activities – watching an internet or TV show, or playing an online game, or reading a novel, or viewing a film, or listening to some music, or catching sight of an animated advertising board at a mall with a particular comic skit about the disasters of house insurance, or sitting with an infant and quietly reading a picture book.

Our own creative writing, whether spontaneous or planned, part of our job or simply something we enjoy doing, is often generated by the things one or other of us notices, things that we do, things that happen to us, events in our lives that get us thinking and feeling. Even when it is creative writing brought into motion by the demands of our jobs or the requirements of a college class it is influenced by our individual contexts and personal feelings. All writing is influenced by its writer in some way, but the modes of creative writing, the options open to us, the reasons for doing it, impact on the dynamics of creative writing.

In short, then, creative writing is a human practice with so many dimensions. To reduce a discussion of it to a few aspects that we might explore mostly through the completed physical manifestations of those aspects leaves so much of the practice, and our understanding, hidden. Of course, doing that does markedly simplify things! If we simply say that only certain completed works of creative writing are worthy of our exploration (say, for example, those things that are 'published', as one set of items) or that what is investigated is determined by the impact of those published things on an identifiable population or the ways in which those material items represent one viewpoint, cultural position, historical moment, technical achievement, makes these examples exemplars of a widely embarked upon human practice, this certainly simplifies things. But it also leaves a lot of what happens in creative writing practice unexplored; and it fails to provide us, as creative writers, with the apparatus, the methodology or even the language to describe for ourselves and for others what it is that we are doing, why, and to what ends.

To compare our discussion of creative writing with that of other human practices, consider how a gymnastics coach's discussion with a gymnast would analyze each component of a particular move, how that move was related to another move and that to another, and so on; and how a set of moves, so analyzed, related to the composition of an entire routine. Imagine you are that gymnast. While your coach might concentrate on certain techniques or make comparisons with other routines by you or by other gymnasts the discussion would be on your physical action, your ways of thinking to inform that physical action, and reasoning behind those ways of thinking. Feeling would not be dismissed, in that how you feel about a move, an effort, a routine, a performance would inform how you craft your future efforts.

The overarching aim of all this would be an understanding of how the relationship between thought, action and feeling produced a desired result. The physicality of the process would of course be a key part of that discussion and, while creative writing is not as physical as gymnastics, this observation is relevant to the discussion here too. Continuing the coach and gymnast narrative, beyond the physicality there would be examination of time, appeal to an audience, aims of each component, goals for coming gymnastic meets, major targets in the months or years ahead, psychological influences, motivation. Perhaps less so there would be reference to theories of gymnastic behaviors, if not direct reference then indirect reference, and these would encapsulate research results into the nature of bodily movements, stress points and conditioning, body aesthetics, and an encapsulating of gymnastic meaning and understanding, along with assessments of current strengths and weaknesses with regard each of the components: the physical, the mental, the emotional.

Only now you have to cry out: 'But creative writing is not gymnastics!' Other than the observation that creative writers imagine audiences popping up loudly everywhere, you are (or my fantasy crying out version of you) of course entirely correct. Creative writing is not gymnastics. It is not chemistry either. Now standing here in the chemistry lab an experienced, and let's make her multi-award-winning, chemistry professor mentors your activities. Some of those activities would be defined as teaching, some as learning, some as research. The mentoring relates to all these areas, though as a strong researcher it is on the new knowledge in the field that Professor A is most accomplished. She's a recognized contributor to the evolutionary advancement of the field, frequently challenging if nevertheless supportive, keenly aware of what else of a disciplinary nature is going on nationally and internationally, a thorough examiner of what you do and what others do and, indeed, of what she is doing. Beyond this centrally strong element of her life, her teaching mentorship focuses on methodologies, techniques, reasons, hypotheses, equipment use, the comments by professional organizations with regard to learning, particularly with regard to core competencies in the field, undergraduate bedrock questions (what's to be learnt), graduate trajectories, projects that these entail, and broadly a narrative of expectation (that is, what needs to be taught, why, and at what level of education). Much of this could be said to be part of the accepted paradigms of practice in the field of chemistry.

Not wanting to give you too much work, I won't suggest you cry out again – but, if you're in good voice you could, because creative writing is also not chemistry. It's not gymnastics, it's not chemistry, it's not riding a horse or constructing a house or conducting a biochemical experiment; it's not archaeology or nursing, accounting, computer science or a theatrical performance. But the salient point is that creative writing involves a combination of the physical, the mental and the emotional, as do so very many human activities. While we can say that in some instances the emotional is less used, perhaps even unhelpful, and in others the physical is all but absent, the combination of these three components informs how we are and act in the world.

There are conclusions we can draw from this about creative writing and therefore about how we can critically approach it and in this way come to better understand it. One short final narrative though, because the gymnastics and the chemistry story were focused, to an extent, on mentorship and creative writing is often a solitary activity, conducted by individual writers in individual writerly habitats. Mentors are often not present, and when they are they are very often not present during the actual writing. That is not to dismiss writerly collaborations, stories of creative compositions in busy bars and crowded train carriages. However, predominantly creative writers write alone and in spaces that they define to support this individual and, by individualizing this way, highly personal practice. We see evidence of this in those biographical studies that create pictures of novelists and poets and playwrights with personalities and practices that are portrayed as (and indeed, might well be) idiosyncratic, most often linking personality to published or performed works and doing the job of creating a hinterland of person to the foreground of disseminated final work or works.

A simple final example of a human practice discussion. Here in my office, let's make it an office overlooking the beach (I'm an architect, and a fairly successful one, I can afford this bright and breezy beach house). In fact, I designed this house, and this home office, with a panoramic view of the beach below and the ocean out front and along the coast north and south, a little brown, a little green, in the distance either side. This is fiction, so I'll take a few liberties, making me established enough and well-off enough to be concentrating mostly on design, though like many in my field I have occasion to be involved in project management, solving design problems, looking at the legal and financial aspects of a project. I am licensed and certified. I spend some time here at home and some in at the firm. I sketch, create renderings, oversee the making of 3D models, talk to clients and contractors and construction teams. Interested in the evolution of my field, I subscribe to the *Journal of the Society of Architectural Practice* and to *Zalt's International Magazine of Design*. I attend trade fairs and expos, almost always the American Institute of Architects annual conference (this year held in New York City) and sometimes the Engineering Architecture World Summit, visit colleagues and previous collaborators in the field, and have a private, personal interest in what I always regard as the connected fields of material arts (ceramics and pottery, site-specific public art) and lighting and display (including image sensing, illumination, safety, and sales and promotion). The discussions I have – both internally, with myself as it were, and externally with others in my field or near to it – are largely about sub-sets of the practices I'm involved in, and often they are involved in too, together with any news on new projects contracted to firms that I know, and on completed projects and in the broad sense of the expression 'how they look'. I keep up to date on the industry because if I don't our firm won't get contracted for much at all – being current is essential to my success. I'm not fixed entirely on the projects I like, but I prefer commercial projects to domestic projects, technical challenges to technical simplicity, first time clients with 'quirky' requests to long time clients with largely predictable ones. Knowing the best ways of doing things with the best materials in the most cost-effective way is something I trade on regularly as a professional in my field. I also regularly take on interns – however, I hear that other fantasy characters invented for this Introduction also have mentoring roles, so I won't even mention my interns (sorry Sally, sorry Arjun, you will go fantastically unsung here).

Of course, creative writing is not architecture. Creative writing is not many, many other things. But to approach it, to critically consider it, to advance our knowledge of it in a way that is productive for ourselves as creative writers and potentially for others who wish to understand what creative writing is, how it becomes, what informs it, and consequently what it brings into the world, the question is not so much what creative writing is not but what creative writing is. Here is an introductory answer:

> Creative writing is distinctive for three combined and inter-secting reasons. In summary, because it employs in a unique way both our imaginative and our analytical capacities in and through writing, and because it creates or, as the word 'create' suggests, because creative writing *brings into being*.

First, therefore, the distinctiveness of creative writing is because creative writing involves the structured and ordered use of a shared and commonly understood language (in the case of readers/writers reading this book most likely the English language) and the inscribing of that language largely into written words. In all types of writing, structuring and inscribing have physical attributes, but they also involve our mental engagement. In doing so, they rely on our ability to understand and to apply that understanding. However, we are talking here not generally about any kind of writing but specifically about writing that highlights and heightens the use of the imagination.

Second, therefore, what makes creative writing distinctive from other kinds of writing is that heightened element of the original, the new and the inventive. Other attributes commonly involved include playfulness, variation and novelty. All these attributes we have attempted to collectively capture by the use of the adjective 'creative' to commonly describe this type of writing. And 'creative' is not entirely unhelpful as an adjective to describe these attributes, in that it does emphasize origination and it does point toward higher level mental capacities and ingeniousness as well as inspiration and sensory responsiveness. However, these attributes are equally and ultimately more productively viewed as key conditions of perceiving of events and things and people in our minds, of our forming of mental images, sounds, activities, our visionary capacities to apply this to our awareness, our acuteness, our thoughtfulness. All these are attributes, and this activity in general, therefore comes about most accurately through the employment of our imaginations, by us being 'imaginative'.

As creative writers, in our writing we constantly navigate between order and inventiveness, between playfulness and analysis, between the recognized systems of our written language and types of novelty and of originality that the imagination produces and supports.

Third, creative writing is distinctive because it is creative in the specific sense of 'to create'. Indeed that is exactly what we do – combining the two first aspects, so that 'creative' in the sense of 'creative writing' is not merely a generic designation. Creative writing is in this way not identical to any other kind of creative activity, even if it shares intellectual and imaginative traits with other activities, here and there. Rather it is a specific creative activity involving the purposeful use of written language and the application and employment of our imaginations.

To critically approach creative writing accurately, to approach it in a way that provides us with information about its undertaking, and about the many results of that undertaking, therefore involves considering its practices and outcomes from the point of view of the imaginative and the intellectual, and its nature from the point of view of the creating, the making, the bringing into being, as well as from the point of view of what is ultimately created.

This is unabashedly a book that begins by considering the actions of creative writing, and that assumes that the majority of this book's readers will spend more of their time and energy engaged with their practice of creative writing than with the critical examination of completed material evidence of creative writing that has been produced by other creative writers. That is not to suggest that evidence of creative writing produced by others is not important, or that it plays no role in our understanding of our own creative writing practice and the results of it. However, in order for your creative writing to happen you had to do it, or you have to be doing it, so the assumption made here is that you wrote imaginatively or are writing imaginatively, or plan to write imaginatively, that you wish to continue to do so, perhaps have a current project or projects, and perhaps will even continue to be a creative writer indefinitely.

The concept of 'exposition' grounds this book with its two primary meanings, the first in relation to the act of 'putting on a display'. This first meaning stages *Critical Approaches to*

Creative Writing as an exposition, or exhibition of ideas about critically approaching creative writing practice. The reason for mounting this exposition is that over time some aspects of the practice of creative writing, and generally of the activities of creative writers, have not been widely discussed or have been considered part of a mysterious, transcendental condition that characterizes human creativity. This notion is supported by the concept of creativity (reflecting its origins in religious discourse where 'to create' was a skill reserved for divine beings) involving reasoning and responding beyond our ordinary human experience, outside of our day-to-day thoughts and actions. Creativity is in this way imbued with a condition of otherworldliness, a metaphysical condition that makes its influence and actions transcendent, arriving somehow from beyond our perception, lofty and, it might even be said, superior. Because creativity has frequently been viewed this way, and because frequently our use of the written word contrasts with this, taking on roles as veracious information provider, organizer and recorder of facts, presenter of clarity and holder of authenticity, which makes the mystery of creative writing even more sublime, some aspects of creative writing have been strangely absent from our critical exploration of the practice. This is the case whether in popular representations focused on the idiosyncratic characteristics of the creative writer (poet, novelist, playwright, screenwriter); in formal analysis of completed works of creative writing where the practical and functional details of authorship are under-represented comparative, say, to the final works themselves; or in texts purporting to teach the practice of creative writing but focusing almost solely on the mechanisms of writing.

This book, as an exposition in this sense, therefore seeks to put on display some ideas, concepts and approaches that explore all forms of creative writing as multifarious examples of a particular type of predominantly written communication, brought about by a heightened relationship between your imagination and your intellect. To suggest by doing this, avenues of investigation that can provide and enhance our knowledge and understanding of creative writing; as well as to consider methods of investigating creative writing that can be customized to each individual creative writer's exploratory needs.

Those learning creative writing, formally within a course of study or informally outside of structured education, will therefore find on display here ideas, suggestions and avenues of investigation that you might not have widely explored as yet. These might also encourage your further thoughts on how your creative writing actually comes about, and how your intellect and your imagination play roles in your own practice of creating with words, as well as how the intellect and the imagination play roles in the practice of other creative writers. This exposition, in the context of being a display, is a manifestation of types of critical apparatus that we creative writers can use in the singular instance of progressing a particular creative writing project or part of a project, or that we can take with us and apply over and over again to the projects we envisage and then pursue.

The second meaning of 'exposition' here in *Critical Approaches to Creative Writing* is that relating to expository writing. Commonly encountered in education, and well-known in venues as varied as academic articles and essays, instructional works and textbooks and journalism, as the term suggests expository writing, or exposition, seeks to *expose*, to reveal, without favoring opinion or adopting a subjective position. Exposition presents explanations supported by facts, arguments made using evidence. Expository writing also tends toward a logical order, though that order can vary. The order of presentation and explanation in this book follows this largely sequential pattern:

Chapter One: Writing with imagination
Chapter Two: Creative writing influences
Chapter Three: Creative writing practices
Chapter Four: Exploring creative writing evidence
Chapter Five: Developing creative exposition

In essence, this pattern moves from the thesis here in this Introduction, presenting creative writing as a distinct form of writing no matter what form or genre you write; through to creative writing's personal and cultural contexts; then to the actions and acts of creative writing undertaken by creative writers; on to an examination of evidence produced by creative writers (you or other creative writers, so that this is both an individual and comparative set of evidence); after that there is a consideration of how we respond and can respond to our creative writing (response, encouraging understanding, incorporating reflection); then to a consideration of what key concepts are emerging in this order of evidence and explanation; finally, to a consideration of how available evidence and your approach to it offers opportunities to explore the practice of creative writing from the individual instances of practice to exchangeable discussions that have the potential to better inform us all about the nature of creative writing.

In addition to the primary sequential structure in the book, the chapters also present a cause and effect narrative in the critical examination of creative writing, whereby action (imagination meeting writing) is influenced, impacts on your practices, yields evidence, this evidence provides material for our examination and consideration, those examinations and considerations provide new knowledge or challenge previously held knowledge. As a creative writer, you test the validity of this knowledge through creative writing practice. Practices, ideas, ways of acting and thinking either remain the same or evolve, depending on the perceived success of the application of this knowledge to your creative writing.

Similarly, the sequential expository structure of this book is informed by the existence of compositional problems in our creative writing and by our seeking of solutions to these problems. These problems and solutions can involve situational knowledge (where knowledge is required to solve a particular compositional issue you are facing on a particular project at a particular time and that knowledge is related solely or predominantly to that problem and that situation) or independent knowledge of a contextual, procedural or theoretical type, where knowledge is gained that proves transferable, applying to many situations with comparable validity.

In both these cases, the practice of creative writing, undertaken by you or another creative writer, is the focus. That focus does not negate others looking at the actions and evidence of creative writing, but not applying knowledge gained from this to their own creative writing or having any intention of doing so; critically examining such things in the pursuit of knowledge about creative writing, for any number of other reasons, including the enhancing of creative writing pedagogy. It is simply to say that any critical approach to creative writing begins and ends at creative writing as a practice – logically this must be so, because that is what creative writing is, a practice.

The book's concluding chapter about developing your own creative exposition is predicated on the idea that we creative writers spend the majority of our time in ways of behaving and modes of understanding that relate to works that do not yet exist. Materially, at least; and for much of our time not in their completed or conclusive state. This state of being, in which our focus is on creating, undertaking, acting to make present, bringing into being is not the same state of being as that experienced by, say, a critic of works of creative writing where the primary mode of analysis is that brought about by the existence of the material object – novel, poem, play. In which case a critic's answers to questions about the work or works, the creative writer or writers, the cultural and personal circumstances of creation, are based on the existence of that material object. While this does not negate the use made by non-creative-writers of the critical approaches to creative writing discussed in this book, it does make the finding of answers to questions about creative writing practice an imperative that uniquely impacts on the daily lives of creative writers.

This book's final chapter, 'Developing creative exposition' therefore suggests we as creative writers need to develop knowledge that accurately informs our actions, knowledge informed by examination of evidence and investigation of definable topics and determinable actions, actions that bring about the existence of works of creative writing but are not predicated primarily on the existence of such works. Whether these works ultimately exist or not is dependent on our actions, and the success of those actions is dependent on our level of understanding of the practice and outcomes of our creative writing. Creative writing is indeed reliant on both our imaginative and analytical capabilities. It involves the structured and ordered use of shared and commonly understood language and the inscribing of that language; but what makes creative writing distinctive from other kinds of writing is its heightened elements of the imaginative, inclusive of the original, the new and the inventive. In our creative writing, we therefore constantly navigate between order and inventiveness, between playfulness and analysis, between the recognized systems of our written languages and types of novelty and of originality. To critically approach creative writing in a way that provides us with useful information about its undertaking, and about the many results of that undertaking, involves considering its dual nature. The term 'creative exposition' is used in this book to refer to the many elements embedded in these critical approaches.

Creative exposition presents a combination of explanations, reasons and evidence to support arguments about our creative textual practices. But critical approaches to creative writing extend beyond textual practices too, because creative writing practices do not only have textual identities. These additional elements include the philosophies informing our individual and societal engagement with creative writing. They include our core writerly competencies around the imagination, cognition, physical actions of taking an idea or emotion and communicating it in inscribed words, and our creativity as it applies to actions of writing. They also involve our understanding of such things as the interdependence of different types of knowledge (creative writers are voracious users of many kinds of subject and content knowledge, in addition to knowledge about writing techniques and artistry); and our engagement with ways of thinking that rely on fluidity and continuousness (in that the imaginative work we do involves memory as well as immediacy, intersecting actions and thoughts, physical movements as well as conscious and unconscious engrossment). Creative writing deals also in personality, motivation, empathy and desire (because creative writers employ personal emotional contexts, attempt to portray feelings in our work and arouse feelings in others, vary in personality and motivation but must ultimately act in order to create). Creative writing requires utility (writing is a practical enterprise, a crafting of something for the purposes of both art *and* communication), and creative writing accentuates the pursuit and consideration of meaning and of causality (when we choose a mode, form, style we surely must understand something of what effect that choice will have on a reader or audience). Finally, creative writing relates directly to lived experiences (creative writing is nothing if not the joining of the creative writer's lived experience, in some way, with that of a reader or audience).

The intersection and association of all these elements contribute to us having a reliable critical approach to creative writing and can enhance any individual understanding of what we each do as creative writers. They can also contribute to the discipline of creative writing as we find it explored, and taught, in education – not least in offering avenues for further research through creative or critical practice, or most often a combination of these approaches. That creative writing is embraced by so very many people in the world makes our greater understanding of it a contribution that extends well beyond education.

One

As a creative writer, you are logically committed to two fundamentals – **writing** (that is, specifically here, 'words inscribed') and to the active use of your **imagination**. Your commitment to these fundamentals is the primary context of your creative writing. In that respect, it is around these fundamentals that all else is built and to which all else relates.

You could, of course, write but not do so with a heightened imaginative approach – that is, choose to write other forms, and to ultimately produce other kinds of results that would not be considered works of creative writing. You could, of course, apply your imagination in other ways, to other activities, to other things, using a platform other than writing (in the arts, or sciences or social sciences). Creativity, taking that word to mean specifically here acts of creating, actions of "bringing into being" and also to refer to its more general meaning of being creative (imaginative, inventive, original, innovative, new) is a common human attribute. We invent (tools, for example, the invention of which has long contributed to humankind's success) and we seek to be original (to highlight our personal identities, perhaps sometimes to improve our chances of career success, perhaps to contribute to the world in an identifiable way) and we often enjoy the new (perhaps because it embodies renewal of our lives or engages our intellectual curiosity or adds to our wealth of experiences).

Our worlds are composed of what we sense around us in the immediate environment, at the immediate time, and what we have in memory, not necessarily in a linear way but in a condition of re-composition as much as recalling. Memory, like the imagination, informs our impression of the world around us and of worlds composed of a combination of sensory information and our remembered thoughts, feelings and experiences. That is, worlds that might be like that around us, but that might also be worlds of the mind, drawing from observations or responses past and present, and in some cases re-working these, or combining them or having them transmute in some way. We are therefore moving between different cognitive activities, in which the imagination, the intellect, our senses, memories, feelings, all play a role. Other creatures might indeed be similar, but what we refer to as creativity, as being creative, is in the most part referring to a higher order human achievement, drawn from the idea of 'creating' having an association with the divine, the transcendent and representing a high level of cognitive function too.

If seeing creativity this way recalls that it is an ability of a higher order, this notion also interestingly relates directly to writing, in that writing too is a higher order activity. The ability, that is, to turn a thought or feeling into a communication that can be recorded and shared with others, and in being recorded can gain some longevity if not necessarily permanence. Writing, as a method of doing that, and a method that has involved the creation of tools of various levels of sophistication that assist us to do that, draws on a vocabulary that represents the nuances and understandings and cultural conditions of our languages, and turns a system of inscribed symbols into a method of exchange within our species. Writing as a method that frequently transcends space (that is location, distance), transcends time (that is, in being an enduring method of exchange as well as a relatively immediate one). Writing as a method that has evolved, through processes of translation and transmission, and through the considerable value we have placed in the practice and its outcomes, into a global mode of communication, as well as becoming an art form (that art form we know most frequently, of course, as 'creative writing').

The two fundamentals in creative writing – writing and the imagination – brought together by your decision to be a creative writer, are therefore, certainly significant in themselves. They have value because we have valued them personally and culturally for their contributions to human life and human engagement with what is observable to us, and what is perceivable by us, and we have done so over a considerable amount of time. But they also have identifiable value in their distinctiveness and in the ways in which they are associated with our human distinctiveness – in other words, in the way we use and view them they are what we might call 'species specific', they are distinct to humankind. And yet as significant in themselves though they are, these two fundamentals of writing and imagination are even more significant when combined, when we consider their combined actions and interactions, and the reasons behind your choice to combine them, how you go about combining them and the potential results that then ensue from your choices and your actions when combining them.

To critically consider the context of these two fundamentals of your creative writing we can think about what they actually involve. Forms of writing and forms of the imagination can be starting points to explore the functions of these fundamentals, to put these functions in individual and holistic contexts, relating them to your individual practice as well as to how forms of writing and forms of the imagination are generally considered in the world. We can likewise consider if both writing and the imagination have systems and structures, or perhaps if writing does but the imagination does not. Or if the imagination has a system but has limited or no structure. Or if in fact writing and the imagination share a few or many functional, structural and systemic characteristics. We can look closely at how both of the fundamentals are represented and whether those representations impact in any significant way on how we utilize these fundamentals. We can consider if (and if so, how?) writing has evolved over time. And we can consider whether the human imagination has evolved over time too. Whether such change has been systemic, and perhaps evolutionary, or whether in the case of the imagination (say) how the human imagination operates is much the same as how it has always operated, with events in its history only providing focal disruptive points in an otherwise perpetual, unbroken story. Whereas with writing (say) change has indeed been evolutionary and constant as human languages have evolved and how we use language, based on societal evolution, has impacted on such things as diction and style of address and viewpoint, punctuation and grammar.

WRITING

Inscription is clearly fundamental to creative writing in that it refers directly to the act of preserving an utterance by engraving, imprinting or indeed by writing (the Latin origins of the word 'inscribing' specifically refer to writing). How we define writing today has been impacted upon by the technological changes in the writing tools at our disposal, changes that we have brought about over thousands of years. If we talk of writing in the contemporary world, we need to incorporate figurative uses of the term 'writing', words typed into a computer, words appearing on a smartphone screen, writing 'inscribed' in pixels. Imprinting today therefore can be more a case of 'making appear' than it is a case of 'etching'. For some time, such virtual versions of writing have also included the recorded voice. The use of other parties to do the physical labor – amanuenses – has been practiced too, and for a great deal longer than we have recorded voices. Although the act of writing is physical, it is therefore not necessarily you, the writer, who has to do that primary physical work. Not only what appears but who makes it appear is part of the constant of creative writing. Practical implications emerge from what and who is doing the writing. That is, many creative writers prefer to write (make their inscriptions) with specific writing tools. Some enjoy the physicality of certain methods of composition – the tactile responsiveness of touching a writing instrument or the sense of order or organization created by a responsive computer program, or the aural stimulation of hearing recorded words out loud. Some creative writers utilize the critical eyes of others, of casual readers, or editors, to make the labor more interactive. How these creative writers transfer draft documents, receive responses, transmute those responses into their further drafting, into revising and into editing, all have a physical presence and pattern, and an impact on the writer – perhaps bringing about a sense of achievement, perhaps releasing something from sight in order to return to it anew, perhaps providing a satisfying emulation of the act of exchange between you as a creative writer and your largely anonymous future readers. Some creative writers find the movement between ways of inscribing useful in critically assessing their progress on a work (for example, a creative writer who prefers to sketch notes by hand but to type a draft into a computer; or the creative writer who writes directly into a computer but prints out work in order to edit it). All this involves individual decisions about modes of writing and your preferences relating largely to the physicality of writing.

Leaving such individual decisions to chance, and our responses to the physical appearances of writing to our entirely personal assessment, is not generally the case. For much of the world, learning about writing, and about how to do it, has been part of the core educational experiences passed on from one generation to another. Literacy, as it relates to understanding writing and to reading inscribed words, and to being able to write in ways that are understandable and therefore exchangeable with others, has for some time been considered an important personal, communal and societal skill indicative of advanced cultures. Whether this perception of the ability to inscribe being a sign of advancement is entirely true or not does not make it any less the wide perception. Therefore, when we are talking about inscription we are talking about a commonplace and observable feature of human life, occurring and often respected in much of the world, and having been this way for many generations.

Writing can refer either to an object or to an action (that is, the actions of inscribing). 'Creative writing' is similarly a term used to refer to the objects of the creative writer's practice (that is the poem, the short story, and so on) or to the actions of writing creatively. Thus, someone can be said to be 'doing' creative writing, 'producing' or 'undertaking' some creative writing as well as to having produced, done, undertaken or, most commonly, written those material objects identifiable as the poem, short story, the novel and so on. This dual identity is a feature of writing, given the concept can always refer to either or both an action and a material object. Critically considering this assists in us recalling that writing's key feature is its ability to record with a degree of durability the things we discover, think, observe, feel and speculate upon in what would be an otherwise ephemeral way. It is not that we have thought or felt or observed them as such. In fact, we have a great many other ways of expressing ourselves, not least in the wider communication of our social groups and in the ways we create modes of exchange based on knowledge, and the sharing of knowledge about the world, about humankind, about our personal and communal experiences. It is the ability of writing to offer a recognized and often revered record of these things that makes it so significant.

To critically consider creative writing from the point of view of that fundamental of writing, we can examine the features of writing and how these relate to the practices and outcomes of creative writing. Writing, then, includes:

- **The symbolic** – inscribed words are of course not the objects or actions themselves but rather they are representations of them. This means that while words have meaning, their meaning or meanings are also dependent on symbolic reference, the effect seen when combining these symbols, and the wider context of the reference. For example, the expression 'a big cat', combines two relatively simple words, but in one context could refer to a jungle animal and in another to a large domestic feline! The word 'big' is comparative, so it suggests some kind of comparison, made directly or one automatically made by the reader of this word, and the word 'cat' is related to a species of animal but not all of them look the same so even just the visual representation is therefore dependent on context and also on our experience of cats. What these words represent carries with it symbolic choices, relating to a creative writer's desire to create an impression, depict the voice of a piece of writing, support a prevailing viewpoint (from the point of view of a mouse all cats are 'big'!), and conform to or challenge or advance an impression, a reach out to a reader or audience that is as much visceral as it is intellectual. Because creative writing is by definition a form of communication and art that is inventive, original and new, the symbolic dimension of writing is in this way intensified. It would be fair to say, based not least on the fact we use education to enhance this, that readers and audiences are encouraged to respond to works of creative writing with this in mind, that it is to creative writing's underlying suggestions, references, associations that we often turn. The symbolic nature of the constant of writing is therefore deeply embedded in how we practice creative writing, as well as in how we respond to works of creative writing.

- **Longevity** – with the durability of writing providing one of its most significant contributions to human life, longevity or the ability to sustain and exchange and contribute to intra-generation and inter-generational understanding is notable here. Writing in this way forms a bond, a narrative of human existence, over time. If this core characteristic of writing is that it has longevity or the ability to impact over time, then a core characteristic of creative writing is also that it is a creative art that has durability. Were we lyrically inclined, we could therefore say that creative writing is a practice of 'etching in time' our thoughts, feelings, observations and ideas, and exchanging these with other humans, some we can know and many through time that we can never know. While we might point to some of the visual arts, including public material arts, murals, installations, architecture, landscaping, even monuments as similarly based in durability, we can equally point to art forms (theatre, for example, music, some of the media arts, dance, material arts using perishable or unstable materials, ice, sand, living flowers and the like) where the predominant characteristic is momentary, immediate and much located in the live event itself. Some art forms sit measurably between these, as durable as their technologies or only as durable as the ability of our technologies to preserve them. With creative writing, alternatively, by and large (though not always) we can talk about the *event* of writing and the *post-event* of the texts that remain well after that event of writing, supported by technologies that have been relatively successful in preserving these texts for long periods. So the practice of creative writing has been common, over time, and the results of it (the objects, the works, the artifacts) persist, and they have persisted over time.

What the longevity of writing also means, therefore, when it comes to writing generally and as it relates to creative writing, specifically, is that works of creative writing represent historical moments. Writing, put simply, is also a historical record, taking into account the tools available for writing, the uses and styles of language at that time, and the occupational and cultural context of the creative writer. Critically considering these things in relation to our own writing practices, we can use durability, and the inscribed evidence of it, to assist us as creative writers in determining the distinguishing features of our contemporary relationship with and use of writing.

- **Being transportable** – writing, in many of the material formats we have delivered it, is most often transportable.

It is movable. We could even say that it is 'nomadic'. That is, certainly creative writers themselves are able to (and have often) worked in different spaces and places. The art form is itself portable, and often has been easily so. The works produced are frequently designed to be carried with their consumers – certainly in the case of books, and in the case of other venues for creative writing (the theatre, the film set, the video game studio) it is accurately not the creative writing that is fixed but the production processes that incorporate it. Our inscribed communications, the art form we work in, is based on movement – even though we frequently find the critical inclination to talk more often of the public performative arts as those occupying discussions about movement and motion. And yet, think of words being written across the page, of the gathering momentum of lines and sentences, the decisions made in different cultures and the orientation of a written page, as words are inscribed left to right or up and down, the flicking of pages, the eye traveling across a paragraph, an entire page. The practice of creative writing, the inscribing of it, *is* motion; creative writing *is* movement.

When works of creative writing are complete, and at times even when they are not, they become items of exchange, sometimes via commercial means, sometimes between members of a community, friends and social groups of many types. This of course can happen in a physical sense, books bought and sold, books lent and borrowed (here occasionally fraught with stories of absentmindedness, avarice and shame), or via electronic means, works distributed by digital media technologies. It can happen by occasional fortuitous circumstance, or it can happen with an orchestrated regularity. The written becomes nomadic, in this way;

and, when it is creative writing, already embodied with the movement between the creative and the critical, the imaginative and the intellectual, the analytical and the emotional, then the nomadic nature of the exchanged inscription further exemplifies the art form with which we are working. Creative writing is in this sense an exemplar of movement. It is about fluidity and exchange and though writing does indeed record, it does print into place, the actions of doing so and the objects created are infinitely transportable.

- Writing is also **encoded** – by virtue of its role as a representation of our ideas, thoughts, feelings, responses and reflections – as a depiction of a generally agreed language, as a series of 'markings' created according to culturally agreed referents, as an historical record (styles of writing change over time) – inscription is encoded. Writing is encoded to carry meaning not only on the surface of representation but beneath it as well. Writing's underlying codes relate to frequently unspoken shared understandings and regularly exchanged human values. For example, while punctuation is indeed a practical tool with the primary purpose of making a communication more comprehensible, think also of the signal sent when a sentence is concluded and the new sentence begins with a capital letter, a suggestion about organization, moving to a new stage of discussion, introducing something, the juxtaposition or contrast of one thought with another. A comma indicates a pause, but the length of pause indicated is influenced by the pace of the language you are using, the nature of silence in the cultural situation, the characteristics of the expression in the social situation envisaged. In general, writing's codes include an implied reference to memory (because to write in an exchangeable way you have to recall the correct symbols to inscribe, to create words, to ensure a thought or feeling can take on a physical textual identity) and writing relates a dexterity (because the shapes and styles of writing point to this. Your ability to use these effectively suggests a prowess). Writing likewise is encoded with a systemic reference to education, to the learned ability to interpret and comprehend, to the processing capabilities of an intellect, and to commonsense agreements on what constitutes a language.

- At the core of writing are **observable patterns** – at least to writing undertaken over any length of text – and in the many ways 'observable' can also refer to an analogical range of modes of perception (heard or felt writing is also 'observable' in that sense). Therefore, we recognize patterns of inscription that have literal or metaphoric identities. Those patterns, while not necessarily presented with the kind aesthetic intent that we find in material arts involving inscription nevertheless recall graphic modes of representation, the patterning we find in other art forms, the natural patterns we see in the world around us, even perhaps the patterns of our lived existences. In this way the patterns of writing suggest a consistency (and, we might say, a 'constancy') with the world around us, with our experiences, and with our responses to life and living. That writing carries with it a sense of our involvement in patterning our world. It suggests we have a degree of control over what happens to us, that we are empowered. That what we experience, in the broadest sense what we observe, is in some way logical, understandable and responsive to us.

YOUR IMAGINATION

As the second of the two fundamentals of creative writing, the imagination has frequently been speculatively examined, rather than being the subject of a firm, detailed exposition. As an alternative to explaining or exhibiting the imagination (its results certainly have been shown and examined, but largely not its operation, its varied methods, its modes of engagement with our external and internal worlds) the approach is more often to celebrate it – not without reason, but largely without sustained and multivalent critical attention. There is an interesting correlation here with the ways in which we have approached discussions of beauty, throughout time. As is the case with the imagination, while there are fields of study that consider beauty (aesthetics, most obviously, but also sub-sections of such fields as psychology and philosophy) the sense in which consensus has been reached on its many elements, or in which such consensus might ever be reached, remains remote. Not only is this a product of such things as different cultural values – as it is likewise with the imagination – different personal backgrounds, varying individual psychological make-ups, the influence of experiences and types and depth of education, but there is an implication that beauty eludes complete explanation because it can, and should, be a mystery. So it goes with the imagination. We approach the imagination much as we approach investigations of love, offering explanations of elements of human chemistry, mental traits, physical attractions, the operation of social groups, but ultimately backing away from attempting to fully explain it. This characteristic of analysis permeates work on the imagination, so that whether in developmental psychology (where the work by definition is on the cognitive evolution of infants and children, and frequently focuses on play and sensory response) or in neuroscience (where the focus is on brain activity and neural circuitry) or in education (where the personal and cultural analysis of the imagination take on social group and civic imperatives), there is an incompleteness that presents itself as part of the character of the imagination itself. As an example of how we celebrate more than critically examine, in 2013 many popular press outlets reported that scientists had 'located where imagination occurs in the brain' (Gregoire, 2013). Like finding the grail of beauty or the code to the enigma of love, there the imagination was! However, perhaps to the connected dismay of dating agencies and those who sell those ubiquitous 'beauty products', much like the secrets of beauty or of love, the imagination was in fact not really 'located'.

To start, the article that set the stories in motion was actually entitled 'Network structure and dynamics of the mental workspace' (Schlegel *et al.*, 2013) – no mention of the imagination at all in the title – and though indeed the work was investigating what many refer to as the imagination it began somewhat more prosaically. It did so by establishing its own parameters, and its own methodology, which clearly were not intended to encompass the complete range of ideals, ideas or indications associated with the human imagination. That article begins:

> The conscious manipulation of mental representations
> is central to many creative and uniquely human abilities.
> How does the human brain mediate such flexible mental
> operations? Here, multivariate pattern analysis of func-
> tional MRI data reveals a widespread neural network that
> performs specific mental manipulations on the contents of
> visual imagery.
>
> (Schlegel *et al.*, 2013: 16277)

So, visual imagery, MRI data, neural networks, consciousness, mediation. This study, popularly embraced as 'locating' the imagination, more accurately was investigating pre-determined elements of it. To do so, it speaks specifically of 'conscious manipulation of mental representations', largely leaving out dimensions of sensation, and it doesn't suggest any possibility of unconscious as well as conscious imagination. So the project, while laudable, was far from a conclusive enterprise, nor by its own declarations of its focus was it intended to be.

Fields of study approaching the imagination are many, because our notion of the imagination in its universality, its combination of the concrete and the abstract, and its positiveness, invites wide interest. Studies of the imagination are more widely drawn than those concerned with beauty. Perhaps in part because it doesn't carry quite the social and personal selectivity that critical studies of beauty suggest, and because imagination is not always viewed as so influenced by cultural or historical characteristics, but as an innate trait that humans possess and that has enduring value – enduring, that is, throughout time and across cultures and in relation to higher order human characteristics and values.

As a constant of creative writing, seen as part of the definition of what makes this kind of writing distinctive, and including an association with the idea 'to create', the imagination can better be critically approached in relation to creative writing by considering its constructive contributions; the ways in which we use our imaginations, and the elements of the imagination that are determinable by concerted attention to how it influences this distinctive type of writing:

- The imagination is **schematic**, offering organizational input, arranging sights, sounds, impressions, ideas, emotional contexts, conceptual groundwork. Of course the schema employed might be fanciful or disjointed or combinatory or speculative, but the approach is schematic nevertheless. While this schema, or plan, might not be actual, might never result in action, and might appear fortuitous rather than well-founded, it provides an impression, an insight that could not have been reached by intellectual endeavor or immediate sensory processing.

- The imagination is **multi-dimensional**, so that while intellect might reason and arrange and attempt to understand by delving deeply into one or a few avenues of thought, or indeed reasoning might construct arguments according to logic or premises determined by their potential deductive but certainly their inductive validity, the imagination works across thought, throughout feeling, in layered and networked ways.

- As its multi-dimensional and schematic nature indicates the imagination is also **fluid**. While it is true that the imagination might repeat, overlap, create a resonance, a pattern that while rhythmically interesting to us nevertheless appears to fix on an impression or to be delivering a recurring theme or idea, or dwelling on a concept or sensation, the modes of the imagination are nevertheless fluid. They are so not least because your imagination is not determining selection primarily by way of analytical relevance, it is less hierarchical, incorporating the influences of personal feeling, the experiential (past and present experiences of sight, sound, touch, emotions), the metaphoric as well as the literal, relating each to another in some way, over space and time, not necessarily linear and not necessarily seeking a conclusion. This is reminiscent of the nomadic nature of writing, the transportable recording that embodies many inscriptions.

- The imagination deals in **factual evidence, alternative factual scenarios and in the fantastic** – sometimes independently, sometimes in combination. That is, the imagination can deliver a factual interpretation, memories largely intact, transposition of sights, sounds, feelings from reality. It can pose, and indeed rehearse or play out alternative factual scenarios whereby the elements are realistic but the progression or outcomes, connections or juxtapositions are alternative, not how things are or were but how they might be. The imagination can also offer the fantastical, clearly unrealistic events, scenarios, things, experiences, that operate as aspects of your psychological, emotional modeling, that attempt to overcome limitations of your experience, or pose material conditions from transcendental evidence, or operate to raise questions that assist in further grounding what is real.

- Within the reach of its offerings, whether in experiences or thoughts or feelings the imagination is **cause and effect based**. It must be so because the imagination has to convince you of the internal validity of what it offers you so that you consciously or unconsciously follow a line of thought or respond to the ideal or ideals it presents. Consciousness we might quickly envisage operating that way, in that it is often considered to involve decision making based on a type of constructed perception; but, unconsciousness is also not without shape, containing automatic responses and information processing. While indeed the imagination can vary in what it offers, over many planes of reference, the causal aspects are part of how the imagination suggests that there are relationships being created, which might even be considered in terms of neural pathways that are leading somewhere, offering some suggestion of future resolution or reward.

- The imagination is **connective and combinatory** – it connects one thing, one event, one observation, one feeling with another, or combines these, or connects and combines simultaneously, not always in logical or literal ways, so that the newness, the novelty associated with our imaginative work is the product of de-connection and re-connection, or unique combinations, or combinatory layering, one plane of reference leading to an imaginative leap to another, much as in metaphor but in the case of the imagination using such tools as part of a more complex comparative method whereby your mind chooses, arranges, presents, and in doing so suggests possibilities, often with a number of dimensions.

- The imagination **prioritizes**. It does so in order to feature those elements of your thoughts or feelings that drive a moment or that seem to offer most possibilities for a successful exploration of an idea or a response to an experience or to be determined via alternatives or to best relate perceived facts. The imagination's prioritization can be seen as narrative-based, not because we necessarily imagine in story form, but because we map much in the world onto the narrative of our lives, beginning, middle and end; and because your imagination seeks to present (and human beings frequently understand through story, through narrative shapes) and because narrative is an account, and the imagination, however much it might adopt a fantastical mode, seeks to offer some kind of account of something or someone.

- **Active** in how it operates, the imagination suggests action, it suggests you are not passive. Even if your imagination is at work while you are physically inactive or while you are not particularly intellectually engaged, its modes of connection, its sense of emerging newness, its arranging of observations and evidence, its fluidity, suggests action. The imagination is active in the sense that it involves action and, indeed, it is active in another sense too because by imagining you are not being passive, you are (even if indeed in your mind) participating in the world, in an event, in a moment of time.

- The imagination is not simply about recording or presenting, it involves **manipulation**. Connotations of suggesting your imagination can be 'manipulative' might seem overly negative, suggesting that your imagination can be unscrupulous. Arguing for the value of the imagination, it might be politic to try to counter such a suggestion, given that it presents the imagination as potentially malicious or destructive, as well as focused on structurally changing relationships, which is what the intention was of using the word 'manipulation' here. But the fact is our imaginations are not morally superior to other elements of our make-up or aspects of our lives. Our imaginations are as ethical and moral or as unethical and amoral as any other human characteristic. So, the imagination can manipulate to create scenarios, scenes, things, people; and someone's imagination can indeed be manipulative in creating scenes, situations, things that transgress our conscious control and infringe upon our sense of self or indeed our oversight of the self.

- The imagination is **experiential**, drawing not only from what is around us at the moment of imagining but also from our memories. How much of what we imagine relates to what we immediately perceive and how much it relates to past experiences, observations, thoughts, is not determined. The imagination works by fluid selection, combination, consideration – not restricted by perception or observation. While we might aim to control the operations of the imagination in a purposeful way – many creative writing workshops and books about creative writing have a chapter on developing your imagination or stimulating your imagination – what experiences best encourage or support or develop our imaginations is not entirely confirmed. There is some evidence that new experiences, stimulating the processing functions of your brain, participating in challenging intellectual pursuits, delving into avenues of knowledge or experience that you have not previously explored, has a positive experiential impact on the strength and scope of your imagination. But how and to what extent, and how individualized these things have to be, have not yet been determined.

- Because the imagination involves becoming aware, in some way, regarding something, someone, and certainly at least somehow understanding and interpreting, even if this understanding and this interpreting is highly personalized, then the imagination can be said to be based in **perception**. You *become aware of* through or with your imagination. You may not sense in the immediate world what you imagine, but you internally observe or become aware of it, you comprehend, whether it is an existence or an action, a feeling, or a thing.

- Finally, the imagination **determines and deals in salience**. That is, the imagination determines what comes to prominence in your mind, that which is not only related to immediate sensory information, or the primary result of analytical or intellectual work, and it prioritizes through its combination of thought and feeling, and determines what most impacts on you, your reflections, your responses to circumstances, your organization of your reactions.

The imagination is selective and while it might be seen as a higher order human trait, drawing on the intellectual strengths that humankind possesses, it is also concerned with elementary embodiment. By selection and salience the imagination makes something or someone become. The imagination makes things, actions, and even thoughts and feelings, perceptible.

REFERENCES

Gregoire, Carolyn (2013) Research uncovers how and where imagination occurs in the Brain. *Huffington Post*, www.huffingtonpost.com/2013/09/17/imagination-brain_n_3922136.html (accessed January 21, 2018).

Schlegel, A., Kohler, P.J., Fogelson S.V., Alexander, P., Konuthula, D., Tse, P.U. (2013) Network structure and dynamics of the mental workspace. *Proceedings of the National Academy of Science*, 110 (40), 16277–16282

Two

We can summarize the influences on and in creative writing by referring to time, place and person. Alternatively we could describe these influences as history, culture and the individual writer, or when, where and who. The influences on and in our creative writing are as many and as varied as there are human lives, cultural conditions and historic moments. As creative writers, critically examining such influences assists us to consider how creative writing is interpreted and undertaken by each of us individually and to reflect generally on what influences any creative writer might encounter. In the spirit of *ipsa scientia potestas est* (knowledge itself is power), that Latin aphorism found famously in Francis Bacon's *Meditationes Sacrae* (1597), a consideration of influences on your creative writing is an opportunity to create a useful topographical map of your creative writing, taking topography to be mental as much as it is physical. In other words, we should view this map of influences as we might view the map of any habitat – with things happening on the surface as well as beneath the surface, things that are relatively fixed and things that are in flux. Habitats, in other words, involve that which happens over very long periods, or appears permanent, that which is cyclical (influences that return at regular intervals, recurring according to a pattern) and that which might be called unique 'events', influences which might only be speculatively predicted in that they have the possibility of happening but are not observable in any permanent way and do not occur in a predictable pattern.

Your creative writing influences, psychological and cultural, individual and societal, are thoroughly entwined because of the way your imagination is entwined with your intellect, in and through creative writing. This entwining does not make the map impossible to draw, but it does mean that we need to consider the influences in terms of their many characteristics and in a way that best reflects the many dimensions of these influences. While it is true that the ultimate result of your creative writing might often be a text – a story, a poem, a novel; that is, a physical written object – the influences on your creative writing are not necessarily self-evident in that physical object, and certainly not all are present in the completed physical work. Influences happen throughout creative writing, at the point of initiating it, at the point of moving it along to some form of recognizable result, and at the point of reconsidering what you have done in order to make it more the type of result you desire. Influences in and on creative writing happen in a way that your actions are a reflection of your thinking and feeling but that does not manifest itself in a way that can be reached by simply analyzing textual evidence. The evidence of influence is available, however, and what is needed to explore it is a way of thinking about categories and types of creative writing influences and giving ourselves the tools to create our own maps of our practice, a thorough consideration of the habitats we occupy.

The following, then, is an exploration of categories of influence on creative writing and the ways in which these might be applied to your creative writing work currently at hand, or to future creative writing you will undertake. This list of influences is indicative rather than exhaustive. It also contains sub-categories that in themselves could be further and more deeply explored. The list is therefore a starting point not an end-point. In the relative absence of concerted critical examination of the multiple influences on creative writing practice, this aims to serve as the first lines on a map that we can draw more thoroughly by an examination of how our individual creative writing happens, when, where, to what perceived purpose, and with what expected results.

TIME

Your creative writing today is clearly not creative writing being undertaken 2,000 years ago, or 200 years ago, or even 20 years ago. Your creative writing this week is not your creative writing that will be undertaken next week – remembering, in considering this, that creative writing involves not only your analytical endeavor but your creative endeavor, where your feelings are as influential as your structured thoughts. Time's influence on creative writing is therefore both the scientific, mathematical idea that shapes and influences our world, and that allows us the practicality of commonsense communication on when things happen and how long they take; and, it is also the fluid, untethered ideal where what is immediately observable is sharing attention with your memories and your imaginative speculations. You are projecting back and forward from a given moment, remembering, imagining, recreating from memory and creating anew. Your temporal perception is therefore a network of different times not one singular, forward-moving, stepped and structured time.

Furthermore, creative writing takes time. Time has to be found, or allocated, or taken from other activities to get your creative writing done. A lack of time is frequently quoted as a reason to not complete some creative writing. Alternatively, having spare time is sometimes quoted as a reason someone did some creative writing. We also replicate and exchange cultural notions of how long certain aspects of creative writing take, certain genres, what effort is involved, how important a work ethic might be generally in creative writing, and what value is placed on works that involve such effort. Length of time is often colloquially connected with the valuing of artistic endeavor (the ceiling of the Sistine Chapel is known to have taken Michelangelo four years to paint. The quality of the work is colloquially enhanced by the common reporting of the time it took to create), and though there is general knowledge that time taken is an arbitrary measure of artistic achievement it remains a characteristic of our valuing of completed work. None of this necessarily is reflective of the real time spent by a creative writer, or the real value created, but the notion of time taken relating to the value or to the creation of value impacts on how we each perceive the time needed to undertake our own creative writing.

Pragmatically, we creative writers actively use time in our compositional methods. We do so more than those working in other forms of writing because in creative writing we have the ability to move around temporally while maintaining or even enhancing sense and meaning. We can use temporal shifts to create effects that relate to theme or subject. Our readers or audiences are accepting of time changes, reflective flashbacks, references made to phenomena, events and persons that are not on the same temporal plane of reference. And we use grammatical tools (such as tense) to ensure a patterning of writing that embeds a clarity of reference and suggested understanding in our chosen mode of communication.

Time in these ways becomes for each of us as creative writers a matter of question and answer, reflection and response, technical decision-making and aesthetic outlook, an element of our art and a tool in our system of communication. In our work, we constantly navigate choice in the consideration and use of time, and how we do this and to what result relates only in part to the day-to-day time with which we are dealing in our ordinary lives. In this way, we could say that the influence of time on us as creative writers is that we exist between two ways of thinking: one where the predominance of scientific time is needed in order that commonsense communication and involvement in the world around occurs, and another where time is more fluid and we direct it, flow with it, alter its course, harness its power to give substance and meaning to our creative writing.

Time in the latter sense is not without its structure, its form – after all, creative writing is writing so it is subject to a great many of the shared formal agreements found in almost all written communication. But our choices in creative writing are greater than they would be in other forms of writing. For many of us, too, our reasons for choosing creative writing as a way of expressing ourselves means that having time and using time this way has emotional as well as intellectual significance for us. Time therefore is a multi-layered influence upon our actions and upon our ways of thinking and imagining. Creative writing provides a kind of empowerment that releases us from day-to-day time. Time for us has more variety, more potential for interpretation and application. With all this in mind, a recognition that there are varieties of time (historical time, compositional time, time reflected in the pace and rhythm of a piece of creative writing, time in the relationship between scene and summary, the temporal influences of metrical patterns, cinematic time as it relates pages or a screenplay to length of scenic time, how long it takes a reader or audience to read or experience a completed work, what is sometimes referred to as 'discourse time' – these to name a few) is fundamental to an understanding of creative writing, and to our creative writing practice and its results. Some other ways we can further explore time's influence on our creative writing include the following:

- **Graphic depictions of time** – gaps in your creative writing text, new beginnings (sentences, lines, chapters), actual statements of time (in other words, the verbal inscribing of time in titles and subtitles or to announce sections). As inscription, writing is physically representational and it is highly symbolic. Creative writing, with its openness to innovative inscription, offers enhanced graphic possibilities. Even relatively unobtrusive line breaks, and creation of gaps are suggestive of the ways in which your creative writing actively manages compositional methods with regard to the depiction of time. We have sometimes seen creative writers take this further, conveying a temporal condition in heightened graphic ways, such as in the case of Laurence Sterne's use of typographical innovation in *The Life and Opinions of Tristram Shandy, Gentleman* (1759–1767), where black pages, marbled pages, and squiggly lines suggest a living text, in the moment, being created as we read.
- **Timeliness** – is also a feature of creative writing, not in the same sense it might be in a news report or a company's strategic business plan or a daily weather forecast, but in the sense that being aware of immediate influences and contemporary creative writing works both to inform what you write about and how you write and to make you aware of

themes and subjects and structural approaches that might be of most interest to a contemporary reader or audience. The latter is of course more important if you plan to distribute your work in some way; however, because it reflects taste, and your taste reflects choices you might make, its contribution to your self-awareness is generally relevant.

- **Time as structure and time as systemic evolution** – informs your creative writing. Narrative clearly has a strong basis in time, relating to a created sequence and to events that are connected or layered structurally in it, to give the impression of time placement and time change. But your idea of time, how time functions and how you use it in your creative writing is also connected to how things work in your mind and in the world. Because writing is systemic in nature (that is, it involves a system of symbols and meanings) time is posed as a communication structured in time and referring to systems of time that change or evolve, internally and externally. Influences here include how structures of time are utilized in the world in which you write (the change in pace of connection and communication seen in the arrival of the contemporary digital is one relatively recent example of influence change), the systemic changes in how time influences brought about by the constant connection and social dimensions of 'social media' are an example of a systemic change in how we understand time.

- **Setting** – which many would identify more readily with place rather than time, is also informed by temporal location, or 'historical time', reflecting the conditions of certain points in the past, present or future. It is created most often in ways that show a pattern of behavior impacted on by time, whether that is in the setting created by the creative writer, or indeed a 'setting', or habitat in which the creative writer is living, which also impacts on writing. Often these temporal locations, one internal to the work and one external to work, intersect, sharing points of reference, even if your habitat, as the creative writer, is not directly portrayed within the completed creative writing text that emerges.

PLACE

Simply, your creative writing is undertaken not only sometime but also somewhere. Influences on it thus include those connected with location or geography. Such 'places' can be personal, cultural, geographic, environmental. Place can refer to the macro (that is a country, a city, a region) or to the micro (that is, a neighborhood, your home, the room where you write).

We can refer to the microenvironments we occupy as habitats. This provides us with a platform for considering the influences of place, or what we can call the ecology of our creative writing habitat, meaning the range and pattern of activities and things present where we are writing. Influences here can include:

- **Tools** – used in our creative writing. While these can be portable, mobile devices or instruments, they can also be used in particular ways in particular locations and relate to activities that are part of our habitat's ecology. So your tools of writing are not necessarily components of a single place but they are objects located in place and used in a place or places, and how their locating and their operations relate to your work has consequences.
- **Environmental conditions** – when we are composing, influence the general viability of us being able to write; but,

they also have specific personal physiological and psycho-logical influences, impacting on our individual moods, or on our ability to concentrate, for example. Environmental conditions enter our creative writing, directly in references, through the stimulating of memories connected with how they look, feel, or affect you, or those around you. The influences here can be on any or all of our senses; they can be the product of topography or weather and climate, the stability or instability of our surroundings. Environmental psychologists study the influence of surroundings on peo-ple, here our focus is on how the natural, made, social, built, learning or technological environments are influenc-ing our creative writing and how they are doing so.

- **Stimuli** – in any habitat can be found or they can be intro-duced or made. That is, habitats are both natural and cre-ated. Elements of your creative writing habitat (let's say the room in which you write) might be mostly made by you, while other elements (let's say the yard beyond your house or the street beyond your home) might be a found environment, as far as it is mostly natural or made by oth-ers. Because those things and events the creative writer experiences actively influence creative writing, there is more open potential for incorporating or responding to a wide variety of stimuli than in many other forms of writ-ing. Anecdotal evidence suggests that in some cases a crea-tive writer might seed their personal environment to spark their imagination – so, the writer who keeps mementoes of particular events in their lives, or the writer who chooses particular art works for the room where they write, or the writer who likes to write to certain music …

- **Research materials** – can be a notable part of a creative writer's habitat – in the form of texts, printed things, published pieces of information. Casual observation suggests creative writers, who deal so often in print also are frequently accumulators of it. However, research materials can be anything. These can be materials you have collected purposefully for your current project or they can be things for other projects, past or future, or simply materials that you found interesting for other reasons but that form the basis of some kind of exploration, connected with your creative writing or not. Research materials in the contemporary world can be largely electronic and accessed in your habitat rather than physically present in your habitat.

- **People** – are often part of a personal habitat, those who are family and friends, colleagues, those you see in your daily life frequently or those you encounter for the first time. In some of your creative writing those people, much as any other part of place, might appear in your work as direct and obvious references, or they might be transmogrified in your creative writing process into composites of those you experience, or selective compilations of personality or physical traits. Their influence could extend to thoughts they express, ideas they share, expressions they use, life stories they possess. Even if people are not appearing and influencing your work as characters, they contribute to your empirical discoveries, and perhaps even to how you theorize on what human beings are like, how they behave and for what reasons. You apply these observations and theories in your creative writing – internally to subjects and themes and externally in considering how a reader or audience might react to your finished work.

Place, then, if considered from the point of view of habitat, influences (and is influenced by) your work as a creative writer – and the level at which this occurs, both in terms of the depth of the influences and in terms of the extent of influence, is available for our critical consideration. As a creative writer, the ancient Greek maxim 'know thyself' is in this way productively supported here by 'know thy habitat!' The influence of place can also be considered from a macro point (that is, for example, a country, a city, a region). In that sense, the following emerge as key elements of our critical analysis of influence:

- **Culture** – the consideration of the ways in which a culture or cultures influences how you write, what you write and for whom you write. The cultural influence on finished works of creative writing has been widely and extensively discussed. Additionally, the influence of a culture or cultures on the life of a particular creative writer or a group of creative writers (those of an identifiable literary movement or from a particular social or ethnic background, for example) has been well-documented. However, from the point of view of the practice of creative writing, the critical approach is not defined predominantly by the artifacts completed or even necessarily by that final work and what is often regarded as the ephemera connected to it. Rather, by the influence of culture on the actions of writing, yours and those of other creative writers.

- **Nation** – because it is a definer not only of many aspects of culture but also of aspect of the economy, education, social movements and quite obviously politics, the nation stands as an influence on creative writers and creative writing. This could be as specific as the kind of funding that might be provided to you as a creative writer through arts or educational funders, and as general as the influence of the nation on perceptions of your place in the world, the sense of national heritage that is both inward-looking and globally comparative. Language traditions are often an aspect of that influence too.

- **Regional viewpoints and regional lifestyles** – are flagged up when we see critical analyses that refer to such things as 'the literature of the American South' or 'stories of the Asia-Pacific region'. These are conceptual viewpoints, and such references to region point toward ways in which there are spatial, cultural and creative dynamics associated with geography, and that these have distinctive influence, political, economic, social and personal. Some creative writers draw extensively on their regions, becoming in effect representatives for them – in the way they use language or the ways in which they refer to regional customs or to regional history. We can think in that sense of someone like the American writer William Faulkner, who had a long personal association with Lafayette County, Mississippi, which he immortalized in his creation of the fictional Yoknapatawpha County in his works. In other cases, region might be barely noticeable in a creative writer's disseminated work; and yet, nevertheless influences their expression, or patterns of their regional lives still influence their practice, their thinking, their imaginations.

- **Macrohistory** – larger geographic entities – such as nations and regions – have a more influential impact on the general political and economic landscape, simply because of their economies of scale for doing so. Your creative writing within these macrohistorical conditions and in these influential sites is potentially influenced by such strong political and economic currents. Clearly, in the contemporary world, global events and notable happenings can be influential even if you are removed from the primary sites of these events and happenings. And yet, living immersed is not the same as simply being informed, and the influences on your creative writing from these large-scale immersive experiences are worthy of investigation, not least because works of creative writing frequently navigate the mix of intimacy and significance. Macro entities circulate the air of prominence, and creative writers associated with them breath that air when they are composing.

Critically examining the contextual aspects of place offers you the opportunity for considering those influences that define elements of aesthetics and genre, grammar and word selection, subject and theme. Living or working in a place or places likewise brings to creative writing the socio-economic, daily life patterns, rituals of relationships and human movement, even the impactful nature of climatic and geographic conditions that are embodied in that environment. All these impact on your creative writing and understanding them enhances our knowledge and improves our understanding of our creative writing practice and its results.

OURSELVES

It might appear overly simple to say that to attempt to understand our individual creative writing we need to individually, and comparatively, attempt to understand ourselves. Although we creative writers might not ultimately understand ourselves any better or worse than any other occupational group, how self-understanding impacts on our work and ultimately the outcomes of our work provides prompts for investigation. This includes consideration of the following:

- **Motivation** – your willingness and continued desire to do creative writing. This might be connected to whether you write professionally or simply for enjoyment; in other words, to whether you are *required* to write or simply *like* to write. It might be related to how adequately your chosen genre or subject matter excites you, whether you have other things in your life that you are more inclined to be doing, whether you find the labor of creative writing at times dull or overwhelming as much as you might find it invigorating. Quite simply, understanding your creative writing might sometimes be being able to state: 'This section here doesn't work yet, because I wasn't enjoying what I was doing that day'.
- **Beliefs** – those beliefs you hold that influence what you write about, how you write about those subjects and themes, and to what ends you write (for example, you believe in personal creative expression and you write creatively mostly because of that fact; you currently believe in the positive possibilities for global communication and exchange, and you write about your local culture with that in mind; you believe in a higher force in the universe, a deity, and this influences how you see human reasons and the results of humans doing things). Beliefs can be personal or communal and, most often, are a combination of both these.
- **Identity** – because creative writing combines many aspects of the self and the self's relationship with the culture and world around you, investigation of influences in and on your creative writing is also an investigation of your identity, or in some cases your multiple identities or your changing identities. Identity can be a fluid concept,

shifting according to circumstance and external influences, or according to changing personal philosophy, or through discoveries, or because of life's impact, roles taken in a family or employment, becoming more knowledgeable about something, ageing. Your identity and your sense of your identity impacts on your creative writing.

- **Psychology and personality** – certainly influential, these too are not fixed, and not necessarily easily accessible to you in their entirety. Some of your psychological or personality traits of course come from your nature, some come about because of nurture. A number of psychologists, and others with interests in particular creative writers or such approaches as biographical literary criticism, have looked at the dispositions of creative writers, their temperaments or predilections. *The Psychology of Creative Writing* (Cambridge University Press, 2009), edited by Scott Barry Kaufman and James C. Kaufman, is one example of these investigations. In this book, as in many approaches, contributors show a general interest in creativity. It is not uncommon to see approaches to the influence of a creative writer's psychology grounded this way. This reminds us that creative writers share our employment of our imagination's empowerments with similar approaches taken by other artists. But, we can also consider how writing, as a vehicle for imaginative expression as well as for communication has distinctive traits that influence it in distinctive ways. These include the relationship between the systematic structure of written language and the fluid methods of the imagination. It includes the ability and frequency of you working between planes of reference, the literal and the figurative, the actual and the fantastical, the observed and the created. And it includes techniques of combination, distillation, selection and shaping that make up the methods of creative writing, where your psychology and personality are involved in the choosing and employing of such techniques.

- **You and others** – as a form of written communication, creative writing is often a channel between you and others and therefore requires comparative understanding. Not all creative writing is destined to be shared, and there is no requirement that all creative writing should be. The notion that creative writing is fundamentally about exchange with others is connected to the idea that creative writing is largely its material results when in fact the material, physical results of your creative writing are only a portion of what creative writing entails. Creative writing does, however, often involve empathy because it frequently deals in what other people than the writer feel, need and desire. Even if it is not sent out into the world in any way, your creative writing is influenced by your associations with other people. Creative writing is also often positioned between the self and others because it relies on a form of inscription that is designed to be meaningful both to yourself and to others.

Your creative writing is different from my creative writing and my creative writing is different from … No need for me to labor this point! Even if the textual evidence looks identical, if we both used the same device, we both wrote on the same subject … even if similarities occur, creative writing is highly individualized. Your actions and results reflect your understandings, your preferred methods, your knowledge, your experiences, your intentions. All this influences how you write creatively, what results you expect from doing so and what results you achieve.

KNOWLEDGE

As a type of investigation of the world, creative writing necessitates you making judgments about what constitutes reality as well as about what is valid knowledge. Exploring ideas, feelings, attitudes, observations, the present, past or future, undertaking creative writing successfully in order to communicate means making some kind of sense (very often to others as well as to ourselves). Because creative writing employs the imagination, this sense-making involves both the metaphysical conjecturing associated with imagination and the bald reality of physically producing writing – that is, creating sets of inscriptions that sometimes become completed objects (poems, stories, novels, scripts). Such completed objects have over time become well-respected cultural artifacts in a great many cultures. All this means that questions of reality and knowledge (or, in formal terms, ontology and epistemology) regularly arise in creative writing. Therefore, a better understanding of creative writing suggests understanding types of knowledge:

- **Experiential knowledge** – knowledge founded on experience, what some might call empirical knowledge, though empirical knowledge is more accurately brought about through experiment or measurement. Such approaches are rare in creative writing. However, knowledge through experience combined with observation is very common in creative writing.

- **Theoretical knowledge** – because creative writing can be highly speculative we could say it is often based on hypotheses, and that it sometimes includes the testing of personal or public theories. You write to creatively explore, to suggest and then test those suggestions, to attempt to make sense of phenomena, to give them meaning and to convey that sense and meaning to yourself and to others.

- **Procedural knowledge** – here a knowledge of how things are done, the human actions that occur to make things happen, in order to be able to convincingly write creatively about them. But also creative writing is itself procedural, involving your knowledge of what actions are available to you and their likely results.

It might well be that part of your reason for undertaking some creative writing is to explore a type or types of knowledge, or to consider what various elements of reality actually constitute. In our critical investigations of what we do in creative writing we can consider how our practices reflect our ontological and epistemological understanding – in other words our creative writing reflects what we believe to exist, or what we can imagine to exist, and it relates directly to the types of knowledge we have, or that we seek to investigate.

MODELS

Because creative writing involves structures, forms, sequences of actions, a system of communication that is the written language, you naturally function as a creative writer with concepts and models in mind. These of course vary greatly, given that you are drawing on your individual background, educational history, range of experiences, psychological penchant for certain things (ways of expressing yourself, what you consider to have beauty, modes of interacting with others, and so on). Some examples of modeling include:

- **Graphic models** – envisaging creative writing in visual, pictorial or diagrammatic terms. Because writing is inscription this is the connected notion of seeing a novel or a poem or a screenplay in terms of its appearance. This doesn't negate your use of verbal language; rather, it points to ways in which familiarity with how creative writing forms look relates to familiarity with how to create them.

- **Mathematical models** – formal poetry is perhaps the most obvious example of this, involving use of length, meter and rhyme in an arithmetical pattern. However, you might use a model based on number of pages (say, for the challenging question of deciding chapter length in writing a novel) or number of pages seen as indicators of time (as often in the screenplay), or geometric shape, or weight and importance as related to number of words, or components of a whole project divided into fractions of that project. This can be more or less explicit, a guide to you as the writer or also a guide to readers or audiences.

- **Motion based models** – envisaging your creative writing as conveyance, a mode of transport for ideas, themes, subjects, event, observations, images, characters – in other words, that your creative writing is a moving object, propelled by the techniques you use with the ultimately aim of reaching an end point that is more or less conceived. Your conveyance therefore sets off and each movement is a contribution to the journey, each stop along the way a stop having some purpose, all on the way to a satisfying destination.

- **Architecture models** – your design for the end results of your creative writing whereby the final 'structure' is representative of the aesthetic you are seeking, each element contributing to the 'building', and the sense of construction involving materials available for composition, the choosing and working with the chosen elements of your design, creating something that is both artistically pleasing and functional for the purpose you have in mind.

Models for your creative writing, which can be largely figurative, can be considered for how you employ them and when you employ them, and investigated for how their employment impacts on how you write and what results from your actions. To give a concrete example: imagine you had a belief and interest in immersive learning. That is, you believe that knowledge and understanding arrive not primarily from the types of exposure but from the depth and length of exposure. With this belief and interest in mind, your approach to creative writing might include strong elements of resonance (returning to an idea or thought or image or occurrence many times, perhaps with different viewpoints or voices or attitudes), as well as graphic evidence of your belief (such as titles of pieces of work that highlight internal characteristics of the themes or subjects with which your dealing) and a pace and length of text that appears as much a condition of your own immersion in its creation as it is in the reader or audience's bringing into the world of the text you create. These would be approaches and results that reflected a model you might be consciously employing. Or your modeling could be unconscious. This modeling could be concerned with the entire project you are working on. Or it could be used at the level of small features of your compositional approach, parts of the work not the work as a whole.

The models influencing your creative writing, metaphoric or literal, reveal the ways you conceptualize the creation of an entire work, or the writing of a line or a sentence or a phrase. Such models might be drawn from fields far away from creative writing, because some structural or formal or systemic condition appeals to you; or, you might indeed use an imitative approach that endeavors (again, consciously or unconsciously) to take a final work of creative writing that you admire and 'reverse engineer' it into your own modes of composition, your own creative writing practice. Of course, not all models influencing our creative writing are available for us to analyze – some are very deeply embedded in the reasons why we act as we do and write in the ways that we do. But considering models nevertheless provides insight into what influences our writing and the ways we might better understand our practices.

The contexts of creative writing – the fundamental and the influences – offer us opportunities for investigation that include exploring textual evidence but also the experiential flow of our creative writing, the ways in which our personal and social environments impact, what we think and feel and believe.

Critical approaches to creative writing are different in this respect to the study of texts and their making from outside the realm of the making itself because the aim is an explanation of how and why and in what ways your creative writing has, and does come about. Critical understanding in creative writing, approached through such a creative expositional approach, begins with recognizing the available avenues for consideration and proceeds by keeping the practices you undertake clearly in mind, accumulating evidence to assist you in making informed and constructive judgements about your practice, as well as providing insights into the practice of other creative writers.

Three

'PRE-WRITING', 'WRITING', 'POST-WRITING'

Creative writing practices are often analyzed using a general three-stage writing model. Those stages are described as 'pre-writing' (that connected to, but notionally preceding, the creative writing project or projects you are undertaking), 'writing' (as the name suggests, the practices themselves, actions and acts associated with the body of physical and mental work of writing) and 'post-writing' (that connected to but following a project or projects). This model is widely discussed in the study of writing, and it is employed to look at what are seen to be the evolutionary actions. In that sense, this model is most often presented as strongly linear, horizontal by nature, one step following another. While not necessarily continuous, the notion is that the parts of the model of the writing process exist as stages in a process and that each of these stages has practices that are largely associated with that particular stage in the sequence.

So, **pre-writing** consists of a deal of preparatory work and this can include thought processing, bringing together ideas, as well as physical actions that might involve graphic representations or associated note making and mapping out. It is said to also involve making choices, essentially choices about the topics you will write about, and perhaps research-ing those topics. Pre-writing is commonly described as a place where reading happens, and perhaps journeys, creating experience of places, things, people; a 'stage' where topics and attitudes and responses are defined and considered. This stage, which by definition, comes first in the process, and because the stages are presented as a developmental sequence, the pre-writing stage is said to contain a great deal that is organizational, some elements that are experimental, and a core of activities that provide a bedrock to what comes next.

Unsurprisingly, '**writing**' is said to follow pre-writing. However, here there is also a curious variation in critical approaches. Some critics certainly describe this stage as 'writing'. Others highlight the word 'process' and this word takes on a prominence that is characterizing. 'Writing' becomes 'writing process' most obviously when the aim is to suggest there is a greater complexity of activity going on, to emphasize that there is a series of actions, to point to there being a range of functions that are performed and that these functions influence the way in which writing occurs.

The word 'process' is frequently used also to differentiate process from product, such as in the well-known approach of Pulitzer-prize winning journalist, teacher and author, Donald M. Murray (1972), and more broadly in that taken in composition studies under the banner of 'process theory'. This stage in the three-part model is generally seen to be related to choices made and applied in motion and exemplified in writing results. The nature of such a 'process' can incorporate critiques of a writer's highly individualized interpretations and actions, or of systematized modes of communication, or of the non-systematized but socialized ways a writer might respond in writing, or of writing conventions, or of the uses of language or of individual experiential influences. These are debated and explored widely, with the aim of presenting ideological and methodological interpretations of writing, both in relation to specific instances and generally.

Founded on the ideal of giving learners more guidance, in 'process theory' how process is taught is of considerable critical interest – often to the point of being the sole focus of critical attention. In this pedagogic vein, those critics who speak of 'post-process' challenge process theories particularly by rejecting the notion that there is a singular process to explore and thus to teach, or that there is a set of identifiable formulas or principles that can be codified and delivered in a classroom. Post-process critics argue for spending more pedagogic time on considerations of how writing embodies the interaction between self and society, individual and culture, through the creation and embodiments of processes rather than of a process.

Whether process or post-process critiques, there nevertheless remains a notion of a stage identified as 'writing', and that this stage involves a predominance of composing actions. Such actions, while certainly layered, are presented as largely linear, heading toward a conclusion that is largely material in nature, a physical object brought about by writing – for example, an article, a report, and indeed a poem, a novel or a screenplay.

Addressing the writing stage in this three-stage model, some have further divided a writer's actions and results into identified subcategories, most commonly using words, concepts and a focus on activities described in their analysis as 'drafting', 'revising', 'rewriting' or 'editing'. Critical analysis working this way assigns methods, approaches and likely results, suggesting modes of engagement through such practices, as well as when particular activities might occur. Usually viewed strongly in a linear way, these activities are said to build on each other, and the definitions of them tend to suggest how these activities both are part of the writer's movement forward in their project or projects and contribute to the writer's sense of what they are doing. So drafting is presented as more exploratory and is left behind as the writer moves to revising what they have now established, and so on to the next step (perhaps editing, to use a common example). Interestingly, this sub-category approach is sometimes concluded with a reference to the activity 'publishing', placing it at the end of this evolutionary sequence in which each step has taken the writing forward and each contribution has largely (if not totally) left behind its previous step.

As the name suggests, following the writing stage in the three-stage model comes **the 'post-writing'** stage. Here a writer is said to assess, critique, return to earlier work with a stronger critical eye, clarify, even focus on some professional writing basics such as checking grammar and correcting typographical errors. Some critics argue for this stage being where the skill of the writer is truly shown. In the discussion of creative writing, there is a suggestion that as a creative writer returns to their writing, and undertakes these post- activities, it is at that point that the imagination is able to work best with the intellect, to utilize its strengths. It does so in bringing to the fore qualities that are in a work but not yet clear. This is perhaps due to the rush of an idea to 'paper' or the laboring mechanics of writing generally or the lack of time for the writer to ponder on how they feel or to develop a depth of response to an observation or an event. In other words, that it is in post-writing that the skilled creative writer spends most time because it is in post-writing where creativity and intelligence have most opportunity to flourish. This showing that while inspiration might generate initial actions, bring about the first appearance of subjects, themes, create a sense of a project in motion, it is in perspiration, the steady, focused, understanding actions of post-writing that the real work of the creative writer takes place. In essence, post-writing is an exemplification of the commonly heard expression in writing studies that 'writing is rewriting' (Murray, 1978).

Critical approaches that focus on the three-stage model, sometimes dealing with it in the sense of steps taken, on occasion in relation to the function of each stage in a complex process, provide useful insights into individual writing actions undertaken. Describing these as 'pre-writing', 'writing', 'post-writing' offers some guidance to the many and multiform writerly actions, in the results of these writerly actions, and in the ways of thinking that underpin them. However, at that point, the usefulness of the three-stage model begins to falter.

In essence, the strengths in the three-stage model are also its weaknesses. The model suggests movement – and, indeed, writing involves movement. This is an obvious strength in the model. The model combines the systemic (systems of inscription and expression forming the basis of all commonsense written communication) with the impromptu and the unrehearsed. That combination realistically captures the psychological complexity of our choices made when writing, and in the interaction between the individual and the social – individual personality, feeling, desire and social interaction, conversation, correspondence. And the three-stage model is teleological in that writing, no matter how disconnected from commercial application or outcome, has a purpose, a goal, an end result of some kind whether that is personal, public, ephemeral or enduring. The model ultimately falters because of its somewhat disingenuous linearity and because of its penchant for a structural and functional determinism, suggesting one thing must ultimately follow another. It considers little that reflects on mind and body in the way these are actually operating when and in writing and proposes a great deal in writing that assumes structures and functions have limited independence and are part of an indivisible generic causal process, irrespective of environment, and mostly of external stimuli that impact on the writer. When applied to creative writing, the three-stage model stalls completely, and though having some positive contribution to make ultimately falsifies as much as it reveals.

Creative writing is distinctive in its ability to 'bring into being', in its capacity to transcend the ordinary world while simultaneously reflecting on it, referring to it, or depicting it, and in its combination or language order and language license, what we might call dependence and independence. If the three-stage model is presented as predominantly linear, and so frequently it is, it falsifies the workings of the imagination, which is layered and heterogeneous, sometimes factual, sometimes counterfactual, sometimes fantastical, influencing writing contingently, irregularly and on occasion fortuitously. If the model suggests one stage builds on another that in itself is not without some accuracy – because, as historians regularly prove for us, what comes before has the ability to influence what comes next. However, absolute determinism suggests an inevitability that belies the way in which invention, inspiration and ingenuity occur – and creative writing most certainly carries all of those traits.

Bald determinism is antithetical to creative writing because such things as human memory and emotion are part of how your creative writing happens, and these things work by association and stimulation, sense and sensation. Such behaviors are not rigidly determined, not predictable by a narrow step or stage model. As critical approaches to creative writing go, the idea that 'pre-writing', 'writing' and 'post-writing' can explain creative writing grows less likely the more we come to examine the spectrum of occurrences and behaviors involved, the roles taken by the imagination and the intellect, the operation of the abstract and the concrete, the factual and the speculative. That all said, I would be remiss if I did not admit that, like many who have written about creative writing, I did once use the stage model myself! Stages in writing are observable, in that a creative writer grows more familiar with a work as they progress it, and therefore builds on this understanding even if this building does involve a complex set of actions and thoughts and responses. However, the stage model is ultimately inadequate in explaining creative writing and therefore is poorly placed to solidly contribute to and improve our understanding of creative writing. We could simply say 'creative writing is mysterious', and not attempt to explain it any more fully, but that would seem to be derelict, given our general human desire to know more about what we do, and why, and to what ends. Instead, not rejecting the three-stage model's qualities but incorporating them into an enhanced creative expository model can assist us. The aim of doing this is to further our understanding of how creative writing is undertaken and how we can come to speak about it in ways that are most truthful. This has the potential to contribute to our own practices as well as to add to our general human knowledge about creative writing. Elements of this creative expository model are based on the concepts of foundation, generation and response.

FOUNDATION, GENERATION, RESPONSE

Adapting the 'stage model' to what we can call a 'typology model', a model based on types of practices not dominated by a notion of there being stages of action, involves acknowledging the experiential strengths in the three-stage model but aligning these more realistically to a creative writer's common practices.

Replacing a discussion of 'pre-writing' therefore is an analysis of **foundation**. Foundational action, foundational writing, or in short, 'foundation', is that which establishes or underpins creative writing being undertaken. Foundation can include elements of observation or research that precede your creating of a work of creative writing. Foundation can include emotional contexts and responses of the creative writer that produce a personal interest in a theme or themes, subject or subjects. Foundation can also refer to your reading practices as a creative writer, some consciously engaging with the evolving project and some unconsciously influencing the project. In these senses it is correct to say that such foundation comes before the work of generating (or generation) of a project. However, this is not best seen as pre-writing because not all foundation comes before: foundational action, foundational writing, and indeed foundational thought and feeling can occur throughout a project.

To critically understand foundation, we need to identify what shores up and sustains a creative writing project – its core ideals, what supports it, how components of it are held up. This we might call the operation of sub-strata or infrastructure. Your understanding of this involves both consideration of the physical and the metaphysical, that which is immediately evident to your senses and that which is not but can be reached via your hypotheses, theories, the application logic (in other words, by proposing why aspects of your creative writing are as they are, seeing if those proposals hold true, proposing why they are true or proposing alternative reasoning). Foundation combines thoughts, structures, forms, concepts, meanings, emotions, values and intentions that buttress and guide your creative writerly action and its results. Some of these things will indeed be established before the majority of your project occurs. But some will not, and they will be created along the way, either strengthening something already in place or introducing something new that becomes fundamental to the project and to its writing. Foundation is not necessarily visible in the text or prominent in the subjects or themes of your text. It contains what other outward facing aspects – those that are perhaps more shallowly present, overlaid or ancillary – are predicated upon. Foundation is frequently to what you refer mentally and imaginatively when considering your project; it is your guiding principles, the concepts, contexts, your writing goals and aesthetic judgments, along with the material evidence that you bring into being.

Foundation is not defined by being fixed in place. It is certainly not always fully developed writing. Far from it: foundation might be notes, sketches, collected primary source materials made by others. Pertinence and congruity define what is foundation in a project. In this way, foundation can be thought of as the essences, the source code that might or might not appear as writing at all, as well as the material groundwork. Foundational practices are immersive as much as they are expressive. Foundation, as such, can come first and then be changed, can be built upon or rejected, can be rethought, bolstered, challenged; elements of it can be proto-writing, aspects to be rewritten but nevertheless providing written outlines, perhaps some initial shape and substance to a work. Foundation can also occur as the result of a thought or feeling, observation or analytical turn occurring *during* the project, at any time in fact before or during the project. Foundation underpins generational action, generational writing, or in short what we can call '**generation**'.

If thinking in terms of the three-stage model, generation would be that described as the writing stage. As such, critics dealing in stage analysis would indeed point toward the idea of the writing process. With a reference to process they would stress the complexity of what is going on, and many would take such noted sub-categories as 'drafting', 'revising', 'rewriting' and 'editing' as ways of describing actions occurring at this 'stage' and the ways in which these actions impact on a project. Each of these sub-categories carries a meaning and is thus differentiated from its fellow process terms, but each also is potentially inaccurate in that these meanings are related to the time of the action rather than a fluidity that acknowledges the role of the imagination as well as the intellect in producing writing.

The concept of drafting is often represented as a tension between original action and continued or fresh action, between established text and any new text, between antecedent and subsequent. In anecdotal ways we see evidence of this way of thinking when we hear reference to such things as 'an earlier draft' or 'a previous draft' or even tell of alarm when a creative writer realizes 'my earlier draft was better than the final one'. These descriptions make drafting a set of correctional acts, segmented in time (that is, quite simply, a 'first draft' cannot ever follow a 'second draft', and so on) and prescribes action to advance a writing project that is measured in the number of segments you have undertaken. 'My novel took 17 drafts to complete'. 'I'm on the third draft of a poem and still can't seem to get it right'. Such an approach belies the ways in which the imagination and intellect are working to confirm or deny your satisfaction with a project, and elements of it; and the notion of leaving behind the earlier in order to move onto the latter ignores the traces of each iteration that influence your thoughts, feelings and actions. By critically approaching writing not as a stage but as actions, and considering types of action and their outcomes, we avoid such falsification. As a critical tool such a typological approach assists us in considering that while we might indeed be moving forward toward a final sense of the work we are writing, something we consider complete, we are not doing this in an overly ordered sequential way, that our writing does not have to be uninterrupted or consecutive and that rather than a tension in our fixed-in-time actions, what might be considered a process, there is release, a movement, a fluidity.

Generation means creating and recreating. It refers to that which builds upon a foundation in ideas, a foundation in written or unwritten form, the physical and metaphysical substructure and infrastructure of your creative writing project. As it is often currently understood and taught 'drafting' does not describe this element of creative writing well. Nor does 'revision' - where the inference is that what exists must be revisited, remodeled, reconstructed in order to make it better, closer to complete. Nor does 'rewriting' - where the inference is something must be physically abandoned and, though not necessarily entirely replaced, in some recognizable way it must be done over, moved from one, existing form to a next, new form. Nor does 'editing' – where the suggestion is of a corrective action, an altering and a refining. Generation, alternatively, refers to the engine of creation, the entwined and vibrant activities of the intellect and the imagination that occurs in your creative writing. Generation recognizes the fluidity of your creative writerly actions, their forms and functions and the results they offer.

Replacing the terms 'pre-writing' and 'writing' and questioning how we use concepts such as 'drafting', 'revision', 'rewriting' and 'editing' is not of course aimed at removing these words or concepts from our vocabulary. Each and all offer some definitional contribution to how we understand writing. However, the aim here is to suggest that creative writing, in its distinctiveness, is poorly served by how we have used these terms and concepts. That in many cases attempting to increase our knowledge about our creative writing as well as about creative writing generally is adversely affected by the meaning of these terms, and that conceptually they very often hide more about creative writing than they reveal. So, what is being suggested here is not that we abandon years of writing analysis, but rather that understanding creative writing involves engaging with how the intellect and imagination are working closely together. Doing this, and using written language, they create a distinctive set of actions, as much as they create a distinctive set of results. Our consideration of this might be applicable for writing analysis generally, but the focus here is to use it to assist us specifically in our understanding of our creative writing.

Finally, then, in questioning the three-stage model and looking for ideas and terms that better describe what occurs in your creative writing, the term 'post-writing', while pointing toward something doesn't quite manage to describe it. Responsive action, responsive writing, or in short '**response**' better captures what occurs in creative writing when we consider what we have been doing and the evidence of what we have done. In other words, response means us responding to what exists or what has been in motion. Writing analysis in the stage model presents overlaps in actions, even recursiveness; for example, both 'writing' and 'post-writing' are said to engage with revising and with editing. Applying the typological here we see overlap also; for example, with both 'generation' and 'response' as a creative writer you might return to the material evidence in front of you. You might also have some new thoughts and abandon some previous ones. You might realize connections between one thing or another where you had not seen it before, and you might reconfigure appearances, structures, representations based on feeling dissatisfied by what you already have in place. However, the stage model suggests a point at which preparations are largely over and reflection has not begun. The stage model posits that post-writing is where there is a concentration on reflection and on such things as external 'feedback'. Alternatively, the typological model presupposes that some creative writing actions can *always* be identified as generational and some can *always* be identified as responsive.

Generational action predominantly initiates. Generation predominantly creates. Responsive action predominantly takes the unrefined and refines them. Generation addresses the partially formed and fully forms them. Whereas generation assumes continuation, response considers an end-point. Response therefore could indeed include wider exposure to the opinions of other people – but only if you, the creative writer, feel there is value in the opinion of other people (some creative writing is undertaken purely for the enjoyment of the creative writer). In that case you might not seek another opinion, and there is absolutely no obligation to seek it. Response can also involve projections of other projects, possibilities that have emerged during your creative writing, but are not incorporated into the current project either because they don't fit well with its subject or themes, for example, or you feel the possibilities are large enough in scope that they constitute an entirely different project. Response also includes an address to the distribution of the physical work, and to the physical (or indeed virtual) nature of the results you might distribute to others. How, to whom, and under what conditions of ownership do you want to distribute the work to others, if you want to distribute it at all? Will it have one identity or more than one identity – as a finished product, as a material thing? For example, as things currently stand in the world, are you producing something for print only, for the world wide web, for distribution on a phone, by a publisher, by yourself, in both a print and a digital form, on its own or with other works by yourself and/or by others, to anyone who wants it, anyone who pays for it, only a small number of people, a certain group of people. Each of these considerations will impact on how you envisage the work you're writing, so although some response comes toward the final stages of a project response is a type of action, it is not merely a stage in the action.

CREATIVE WRITING SYNAPSES

Practices in creative writing work through synapses. That is, through points at which your imaginative and intellectual capacities spark, create ideas, produce writerly actions, suggest in their interaction, association and ultimately exchange such things as genre, form, structure, subject, theme, at a macro level, and everything from word selection to image or metaphor at a micro level. Synapses, as nodes or conjunctions are present in other forms of writing, but it is the heightened relationship between your imagination and your intellect that makes these so significant in creative writing.

At such points, as your imagination and intellect come together, as they must to create both recognizable communication and the art we know as creative writing, your practices become one or more of foundation, generation and response. While certainly a creative writing project might see a predominance of foundation at its commencement and a predominance of response in its conclusion, throughout your creative writing actions take place that can be critically examined in terms of the three primary identities in creative writing practice.

Synapses create a union, or a coming together, and this too can provide us with information on how a project has caught your attention, begun to form, and ultimately been empowered. In fact, the scientific use of the term 'synapses' refers to an electrical cellular energy and that fact is figuratively useful in considering the synaptic nature of your creative writing. It is the energy contained in and harnessed by creative writing that both excites the creative writer and attracts an audience for any finished work, if it is distributed to others. It is the bringing together, in that synaptic way also, of the writer and the audience for the written work – not only because pieces of creative writing contain information, knowledge, understanding to be exchanged but also because they contain human emotions.

Creative writing therefore works connectively. It works through a fluidity that allows different types of knowledge and understanding – the public and observable, the personal, emotional, qualitative, propositional – to be drawn upon and to influence your writing. Some of this can be on the surface of your writing, appearing as direct references to things and experiences, but some is indirectly referenced as it influences how you represent things, people, circumstances.

That creative writing makes sense and displays meaning that can be personal and/or public is determined not by whether what is presented in it is correct, necessarily, or agreed upon through the means of logic or reasoning, but that it appeals to those who encounter it – whether those encountering it are only the creative writer who created the work, or an audience of millions.

The practices of creative writing are more varied than those found in other forms of writing, because of the discursive influence of the imagination, but more structured and intentionally determined than those of many other creative practices, because of the demands of our written language. Creative writing practices are physical – the actual physical act of inscribing, of writing – and mental; they are personal and they are cultural. To understand creative writing, and to gain greater knowledge about creative writing, both our own and that of other creative writers, we most productively can begin with a consideration of the actions of foundation, generation and response, and then turn to the evidence these leave for us to examine.

REFERENCES

Murray, D.M. (1972) Teach writing as a process not product. *The Leaflet* (November). Reprinted in V. Villanueva and K.L. Arola, eds. (2003) *Cross-Talk in Comp Theory*, 2nd ed. Urbana, IL: National Council of Teachers of English.

Murray, D.M. (1978) Internal revision: A process of discovery. In C.R. Cooper and Lee Odell, eds. *Research on Composing: Points of Departure*, 1st ed. Urbana, IL: National Council of Teachers of English. 85–104.

Four

EVIDENCE, WHAT EVIDENCE?

Many examinations of creative writing concentrate primarily on its final textual results. If attempting to examine other evidence they relegate that evidence to the position of ephemera, interesting primarily as background to the final textual results. The reasons for the predominance of such final product analysis are simple: they are the result of the growth of a market for works of creative writing, beginning with the Industrial Revolution creating the means of production for manufacturing such works in volume. This has been enhanced further by an increase in literacy in much of the Western world, and by the professionalization of fields of critical textual study, such as the founding of the professional study of English literature, emerging out of the study of classics in the late 19th century.

The growing market for products of creative writing was supported by advancements in manufacturing practices and greater access to transport. Underpinned by new modes of mass production and mass distribution, propelled by advertising, such changes encouraged and advanced consumerism. Ultimately, the birth of the contemporary leisure class, whose interests have extended to education and to the arts, and generally to social signifiers connected with lifestyle, fed interest in the purchase and discussion of literature and the questions of taste and discernment associated with it. As a skill with social status, as well as a leisure activity, reading and the availability of material to read, fueled by this discussion of taste and discernment, has supported the focus on material textual results. This is the case even today when choices of textual materials to consider is so much broader, diverse and potentially even virtual.

For all these reasons, it makes sense that the physical results of creative writing, the 'product' brought about by us doing it, and the ways in which that product we create is valued and understood, has been the main focus of the critical analysis of creative writing. Such examinations contribute to our understanding of both action and material result, and they assist us in our considerations of *why* and to an extent *how* works of creative writing come about. These examinations are given additional depth by biographical and autobiographical studies that provide us with insight into the lives of creative writers, insights that can indeed inform us about the circumstances of creative writers and suggest ways we might consider our own circumstances.

Yet, as creative writers, we know even more so that in reality the evidence of our creative writing is always multi-faceted, always a combination of factors: our observable actions, material objects (for example, notes, drafts, reference works, visual and aural materials, published texts), evidence of our interactions with other humans. That neither final texts nor life studies on their own can reach that practice and put its many outcomes in most productive view. We know that that the final textual results are only a part of an extensive range of actions and results that form and inform our writing experience. To reach any true sense of our how our own creative writing comes about we must at very least acknowledge the range of evidence we produce, consider its value, its type, its contribution to our knowledge, and give attention to how such evidence can inform how we understand our practice.

ASSESSING VALUE

For our purposes as creative writers, the critical assessment of evidence of our creative writing begins with an acknowledgment that we spend the majority of our time in the writing of works, in creating, imagining and inscribing and less time in our admiration of the final results of doing these things. This is not to devalue the aesthetics or the significance in terms of representation and human exchange of finished works of creative writing – ours, and those of other creative writers. These play a role too in revealing thoughts, emotions, concerns, beliefs, knowledge, perceptions and passions. Nevertheless, simply, as creative writers we are 'in motion', our acts of imagining and inscribing fundamentally flowing, often dexterous, and the focus of our attention clearly on movement. Ours is networked and synaptic activity, where our experiences, actions, engagement with and material evidence of our actions interact, spark off each other, passing imaginative connections and our reasoning across plains of reference. We can most productively begin our assessing of this evidence by considering the value of identified elements in our practice. Such focuses as these assist in doing that:

- **Revelation** – does the particular piece of evidence reveal something we have undertaken, a practice, and in what ways does it reveal it? In other words, the evidence has some value connected to its revealing of an action you have undertaken or a set of your actions that relate in some way to each other. Additionally, what is it that it reveals about that action or those actions? For example, your trip to Cape Canaveral, the leaflets you collected at the Kennedy Space Centre there, and your purchase of a book about the Apollo space program, relate directly to gaining knowledge about the subject of your novel (about the life of an astronaut). Your pictures of the landscape of nearby Merritt Island generated thoughts about lushness and your emotional response to that (which was that the lush can also be overwhelming) influenced your choice of a more ornate prose, a more introspective viewpoint. This critical investigation is not simply a case of tracing back connections to subjects and themes. Such focus on revelation also relates to your assessment *choice* (What are your modes of choosing? How do things, experiences, people pique your interest and become part of your creative writing?), *application* (How does your engagement with particular experiences, things, people become part of your actions of composing a work or works), and *influence* (What, if any, are the notable variations in influence, stronger or weaker, fleeting or more consistent?).

- **Role** – what role did (does) this piece of evidence play in your practice? Is a piece of evidence related mostly to what is called here 'foundation'? Or is it related to 'generation'. Or to 'response'? The evidence might have informed your imagination or intellect, or both. Or it might be doing so as you consider it – the critical investigation of your creative writing can indeed take place as you are undertaking it, not only after you have undertaken it.

Let's say the evidence you're considering is a description of a room where a character is sitting – and you have now produced, it appears, five different versions of this description to be included in a short story on which you are working. Critically considering these you see that you had moved progressively away from complex and compound sentences to simple sentences; that you had refocused attention from color in the room to the movement of light across it; and that you have reduced to almost none the number of sentences starting with articles or pronouns, instead favoring adjectives, nouns and verbs.

Your evidence here has a role in revealing to you how you are using grammar, as well as showing your pursuit of definite meaning (that is, your decision to move attention from color to light reflecting your feeling that you'd like to make a plainer distinction between characters' opinions in the story). It also provides you with an insight into the process you used to strengthen a piece, in this case combining a re-thinking of content with a working of the passive/active balance of your sentences (shifting to concrete and active openings) but retaining the use of description rather than shifting some or all of what you are doing to exposition, for example. It might be the role of the evidence you find is not literal but metaphoric, deepening the ways in which you are imagining or investigating something, in and through your creative writing. So, say, your personal enjoyment of cooking might not mean all the poems you write are about meals, but it does mean you often write with the metaphoric notion of 'combining ingredients' in mind. Understanding how you do that helps to build the strengths of that approach and might also reveal its weaknesses. Evidence might relate to structure or form – so, as hypothetical examples, your consideration of varieties of architecture and the courses you took on literary theory respectively give you material evidence of successful structures and examples of how hypotheses about structure are created. An experience you have might determine the viewpoint you have chosen or an observation you make might define how you approach a theme. Looking at evidence of your creative writing you might discover something as fundamental and basic as when you decided to refocus or reimagine a piece of work. Your evidence here (say, an earlier draft, or a note, or a file with material downloaded on a particular day at a particular time) shows compositional choices that are generational, evolutionary and individual in nature. This is your creative writing in motion, at work, as you undertake it. Like anything in creative writing this might not be a linear aspect – it could be your evidence shows a horizontal movement rather that a forward facing one, so that the refocusing or reimagining is revealed to have shifted your poem, or story, or screenplay or the like into an alternative approach. This being not so much moving forward as moving sideways as the network of activities that inform your creative writing, that influence your imagination and/or your intellect, interact.

- **Comparison** – has the evidence you investigate – in your own creative writing or in relation to the creative writing of others – any comparative value? So, you find evidence of your imaginative leaps, the way you choose words, your patterns of composing – can you compare these with the actions of other writers? An example: some creative writers actively avoid reading similar works dealing with similar subjects or themes while they are writing in order to keep their own explorations distinct; other creative writers have a range of works they draw upon or seek out particular works while working on particular projects. While neither of these might be considered an act of inscribing, the different choices made are certainly acts of creative writing, part of a set of actions you or other creative writers have employed. Other comparative information might be found in formal or informal education; that is, in workshops or simply in conversations between creative writers – what might be called 'craft conversations', where you exchange anecdotes and find you have similar or different approaches. Cross-arts or cross-disciplinary comparisons might provide evidence of action or theories about methods or evidence of how form or focus or pace of creating results might occur, or even how others assess evidence of their own non creative-writing practices. So, looking at how a chemistry researcher conducts an experiment or how an anthropologist seeks out information on attitudes of certain peoples, can offer a creative writer comparative understanding of the actions undertaken, the reasons for them, and the results produced by them.

Comparative consideration of evidence – and the range of evidence available to us is varied and considerable – can also reveal the distinctiveness of creative writing practices, and additionally contribute to your understanding of how your own practices are unique or similar to those of others in the world. By doing this comparative study offers the opportunity to identify the strengths and weaknesses of our approaches, to evaluate how success and failure is viewed by others in creative writing and in other fields, and to consider the human context of what others have undertaken in light of our expectations for our own creative writing.

COLLECTION METHODS/ANALYTICAL TOOLS

To explore evidence of creative writing we need not only to consider what evidence of it has value, and what kind of value, and to what degree it has value and for what purpose it has value, we also need collection methods and analytical tools. If we turn to other fields of human endeavor – many of which appear notably in our institutions of higher learning – we often find developed methodologies, frequently specific to those fields, sometimes drawing from wider domains of analysis (a domain being an area of human knowledge) and developed over some time. The methods seen in the analysis of creative writing are not as well-developed, at least not in their specific methodology, and are also nationally defined according to how creative writing has appeared in particular national higher education systems. Predominantly, the methods used to analyze evidence of creative writing, globally, have been drawn from the fields of literary study or from writing or composition studies (largely in the USA), with the literary studies methodologies, theories and practices most prevalent. The suggestion here is that while these predominant methods have been useful they have been incomplete and not bespoke, and in that sense have failed to adequately provide a comprehensive and productive set of methods and tools.

Considering evidence of creative writing can therefore better be undertaken by determining collection methods specific to the endeavor and then employing tools that reference the actions undertaken and all the results possible. Collection methods thus include:

- **Mapping** of evidence left by you as a creative writer, using this in a specific way in one project or in a comparative way to look at your composition methods, and the influences seen on your imagination and/or intellect over time and over a number projects.

- **Action research** in that you can undertake projects with a prior sense of what you seek to achieve and use the 'practice-led research' to determine what you encounter in the process, the successes and failures, the discoveries, the obstacles in creation, the aesthetic and conceptual ideas, the challenges, the results, considering all of these in terms of your objectives.

- **Secondary sources** and how these are used can provide a resources database that identify influences, the point at which those influences occurred, perhaps how much you valued those influences (according to the volume of materials and their focuses) and to what extent those secondary sources were or are continuing to influence your imagination or intellect (in other words, the fluidity of creative writing suggests a source of information or creative speculation might not simply influence one creative writing project but, rather, a number).

- **Primary sources** might include those not directly connected with a project (that is, events, actions and materials accessed prior to undertaking a project and with no sense they would be connected to it) and those consciously sought out during a project. Because creative writing does not begin simply at the point of inscription, a consideration of those experiential and texture materials that acted as primary reference points, experienced firsthand by you, contributes to your evidential collection methods.

- **Written materials** created by you at any stage of your creative writing forms parts of your collections methods. It might be that, when endeavoring to become more aware of your practices and their results, that your collection methods begin to include saving more of your draft materials, notes, emails, texts, paying more attention to what these written materials represent and preserving them for consideration during and after you complete a project. In doing so, there is at least a reasonably believable suggestion that enhancing your critical approaches to creative writing can also *alter* your approach to creative writing and, indeed, perhaps even alter the results of your creative writing. No suggestion is made here that doing so is without conse-quences – which you might view positively or negatively, according to how pleased you are with your current modes of creative writing and the results seen because of them.

The consideration of evidence of creative writing also involves the establishing and using of **analytical tools** that have the potential to provide the most accurate information. Like any endeavor, the notion of the right tool for the job at hand guides how we consider this. Some analytical tools, depend-ing on the evidence you consider can include the:

- **Descriptive** – describing the evidence you find, and what that evidence appears to represent in its impact, influence and/or appearance in your creative writing. The analysis here is exploratory, and also works as a typological grid, determining what kinds of evidence you produce when writing creatively and by doing so what types or choices and roles for things you interpret to be significant in your creative writing.
- **Textual** – analyzing the texts you find – and this can influ-ence visual and aural texts as well as written texts – by considering what types of texts these are, their rhetorical shapes, and the ways in which these texts relate to the text you are creating. In this case, therefore, the analysis might consider parallels and contrasts in the actual structural,

formal, grammatical conditions you produce and you draw upon; it might consider the cultural or social contexts and/or the way in which these texts have been (or will be) distributed. Your textual analysis might include attention to content, meaning, why the text(s) exist in the first place, who authored them, what was their intention in authoring them, the concrete and/or abstract ideas they contain, the veracity of the texts, their bias.

- **Qualitative** – not all evidence of your creative writing is valuable to you. One analytical tool you can employ is the valuing of evidence or the evidence trail. Throughout creative writing involving foundation, generation and response different events and things carry different levels of influence and of impact on your writing. This can involve localizing your analysis – so that it might be that the book you bought to read for your previous project was ultimately not influential in its creation but became influential in your current project. Qualitatively, therefore, evidence of your creative writing has both project-specific and time-specific elements.

- **Quantitative** – simply, evidence carries differing degrees of weight. This is not necessarily based on volume of evidence, or on what part of your creative writing it was that this evidence proved influential. Assessing the quantitative aspects of evidence means determining how your creative writing project emerged, evolved and came to a conclusion. Within that pattern of activities where is the evidence having greater significance, and is that significance continuing or restricted to the single project you were (or are) undertaking? Quantitative analysis can also be comparative, showing a predominant pattern of your writing behavior at a time in a place.

- **Causal** – what did the evidence cause to occur? Did the visit you made to the museum cause you to reference a piece of history in a certain way in your poem? Did the day you were ill cause you to consider how it would be if the character in your screenplay was suffering from an illness? Causal links offer a way of tracing a set of subjects or themes, their interaction, and your way of representing them.
- **Inferential** – while the evidence is present how it played a role is not directly obvious. Defining your analysis as inferential is a way of saying that some analytical tools you employ are those of speculation. Speculative reasoning encourages contemplation while not necessarily leading to any firm conclusions. The inferential approach you take might draw on a relatively small set of occurrences in your creative writing – say you notice that you favor the use of certain character traits for characters used in your novel writing – to test a theory that you are drawing your characterizations entirely based on people you know socially.
- **Predictive** – you have seen that throughout your time as a screenwriter you have always begun to write a screenplay by writing a short story about the subject and theme first. You believe that your methodological preference for doing this is related to your commitment to narrative cinema and to the shape of the realist short story whereby each event or character resembles those in real life and will influence how you approach your next screenplay writing project. This basic information means you can pay attention to the shape of the short story you write with the idea that it is actually working much like a film treatment.

CRITICALLY USING EVIDENCE

Evidence of your creative writing can take numerous forms – many of these forms not textual, many related to actions you have undertaken that are not necessarily recorded at all. Being aware that before, during and after you undertake a project there is evidence related to it that you are creating and with which you are actively engaging is certainly the beginning of a more aware creative writing practice. Certainly also, there is that change such increased awareness will change how you write – for better you might say, or for worse (perhaps if you believe that an over-awareness of your practice will make you more tentative about it). But the chance exists, either way. How you use evidence of your creative writing, should you choose to engage with it becomes the final question here.

One way you might engage with the evidence of your creative writing is by testing theories or hypotheses you have about your creative writing – things that you have observed over time, perhaps, but have never confirmed. For example, is it really the case that you draw extensively on events or people from your childhood? Do you really favor a certain pattern of description and exposition? Are you really inclined toward certain sequences of action in your plays? Testing theories could lead to you challenging them by attempting other modes of creative writing or to you strengthening your methods by confirming how you write and then considering what advantages your methods might have.

Engaging with evidence can also result in you producing what might be called a series of 'evidential codes' – that is, criteria that you recognize in support of your creative writing that carry certain qualitative and quantitative elements. Coding these, you might conclude that some things you do are 'background', some you decide to call 'support', other elements you consider 'propulsion' or 'the engine' for a particular work or works. Establishing such evidential codes could assist you in being more confident about your process and more inclined to work to improve it.

You can use evidence of your creative writing to look at sequencing in your creative writing and while it might be that the structural conditions of foundation, generation and response prevail as the overarching method of working, understanding likely sequences of practice allows you to prepare for periods in the compositional life of a project. In this way, you might even be released somewhat from a concern that you are adrift and unlikely to complete a project, or this might reassure you when you are unsure whether your decision to shift the project horizontally into a different theme or subject might completely undermine it, or it might suggest a timeframe for the project, because you have long realized that you spend more time in working up drafts than in re-working them, so you know that sequentially when a complete draft is seemingly nearing its completion you are also likely nearing the completion of the project in its entirety.

Finally, critically using evidence of your creative writing provides support for your reasoning and such reasoning gives you confidence in and connection to your knowledge. While it is true that in creative writing we are dealing with the heightened influence and use of the imagination it is not true that the imagination is entirely and always fantastical or speculative. Your imagination is schematic and multi-dimensional as well as fluid. Your imagination deals in factual evidence and alternative factual strategies as well as in the fantastical. Your imagination is cause and effect based so that it reacts as well as creates, it draws upon concrete observation from abstraction. Your imagination is connective and combinatory and it prioritizes. It determines saliences and it manipulates and it actively draws on your experiences and perceptions. With all this in mind, evidence of how your imagination is working or has worked in your creative writing is as relevant and as substantial as evidence of how you have critically, intellectually engaged with topics and subjects and themes and ideas and observations. To show reasoning that incorporates evidence of the workings of your imagination provides you with a critical awareness that can accompany and embrace the ways in which you have used the physical and systemic conditions of writing, of inscription, for your creative explorations.

Five

INVESTIGATING CREATIVE WRITING

The term 'creative exposition' refers here to critical, investigative approaches specifically focused on the exploration of creative writing. It combines the idea of 'displaying' the discoveries you make, revealing truths, with the idea of determining accurate 'explanations' – both of these elements are supported by facts about creative writing drawn from available evidence.

The aim of creative exposition is to increase understanding about how creative writing happens, what informs it, what propels it, what contributes to it, how and in what ways. The most likely scenario behind creative exposition is that you – as a creative writer – are seeking further knowledge of your own practices in order to improve your likelihood of success in whatever creative writing project or projects you are undertaking. Reasons for undertaking creative writing are as varied as are the creative writers in the world. They range very generally from intentions related purely to self-expression to those connected with commercial and professional needs, from the exploring of imaginative fantasies to the creative address of real-world issues, histories and persons. Among all this, there is creative writing undertaken in a variety of circumstances – in the pursuit of education (perhaps connected with inventive exploration of a topic or observation or thought, or with the pursuit of improved literacy or with cultural exchange of a kind that connects empathetic connection with intellect response); in the engagement with friends or family, whereby a work or works of creative writing assists in bonding and exchange within the group; in the creation of one or more of the outputs of the creative industries (in publishing, film, media, games and leisure software, theatre, music, advertising, design, even architecture).

Critical Approaches to Creative Writing is premised on the notion, then, that it is a book being read largely by creative writers seeking knowledge that will inform their (your) practices and relate to the outcomes they (you) have in mind. However, as a long undertaken and widely appreciated practice, our human interest in creative writing, both in its results and its practices, is not restricted to creative writers. In fact, because so many societies regard the ability to write and to read, along with the ability to be creative, as indicative of the advancement and maturity and strength of their communities, creative writing garners considerable cultural acclaim and sustained recognition. This in addition to its important role in many successful creative industries, from publishing to the media, theatre to leisure software and more. With this in mind, creative exposition might be undertaken by creative writers or by non-creative writers. Its outcomes might be applied to works being created, or to the knowledge of practices and outcomes of creative writing from the point of view of understanding much admired cultural products and the methods of creating them. Considering the reasons for your investigations is the starting point for deciding on methods and indeed on projecting outcomes. For example, your creative exposition might aim to:

- **Resolve an already recognized compositional problem** – in building on the foundation of a piece of work you are creating, you feel something isn't 'working', the viewpoint, the sense of time or place, the address to the reader, so you seek to influence the generation of the next iteration of the work by exploring the compositional problem you've identified.
- **Comparatively explore an understanding of final results** – that is, say, you might seek to determine how poets most frequently incorporate their empirical observations into their writing, and how they do this, beginning with textual analysis of final works and then using interviews and creating a typology and then characterization of responses.
- **Determine the next move toward progressing a project** – by looking over evidence of previous creative writing projects you have undertaken, attempt to discover steps that can move your current project to a final responsive stage. For example, the screenplay you are working on appears too static, too cerebral – you know you've experienced this conundrum before, how did you overcome it?
- **Look for observable structural characteristics in your creative writing** – with the idea of attempting something new, something not yet attempted, to see if you can discover more usable options, modes of expression that can be successfully used in one instance or another.
- **Culturally consider the influences of time and place** – to gain a greater understanding of how these are influencing themes and subjects in your creative writing; and, by doing

so, offer opportunities for designing research that deepens, challenges or re-confirms how these elements of habitat are at work in your creative writing.

- **Track compositional causal patterns, based on evidence** – between your imaginative and intellectual endeavor, so as to determine the ways these modes of engagement interact, and to consider if their interaction is to the greatest benefit in producing successful works of creative writing.

- **Examine modeling techniques** – in this case through pedagogic practices, exploring with a class and its individual members how particular creative writing schematic models – for example, graphic, mathematical, models based on movement, on journeys – might be used to explore topics and ideas. Using the group to explore correspondence and contrast, to consider how certain models appeal to one or other of the group, to investigate how such techniques as resonance and juxtaposition, changes in pace and rhythm influence the appeal (or lack of!) of a work of creative writing.

Many of these examples have practical application. Logically so, because they are connected with the action of creative writing, a creative writer's actual undertaking of it. When you are a creative writer employing creative exposition, there is most often an expectation of achieving a positive outcome for a particular situation – what I have referred to elsewhere as the development of situational knowledge (Harper, 2013). Situational knowledge is developed, and indeed needed, to approach questions, challenges and complications in the practice of creative writing, as well as to recognize imaginative opportunities. Such knowledge can be as varied as discovering ways metaphor can deepen understanding by layering frames of reference or how to structure screenplay dialogue so that action carries the force of words without needing an over-abundance of adjectives or how to create character through idiom, or ways of making pace tell a story or methods of including historical fact without reverting to didacticism. In other words, situational knowledge is knowledge gained in the situations encountered in creative writing, knowledge that can thus be applied in the situations encountered in creative writing. Sometimes through creative exposition there is the creation and/or accumulation of more generally applicable knowledge, this also adds to forms of understanding that are transferrable between projects. For the non-creative writer, creative exposition can develop a greater familiarity with the practices of creative writing, particularly those beyond the final published or performed text, so that the evidence explored is more extensively considered and each element of it recognized within a network of connected actions and understandings.

That said, including the practice of creative writing in your creative exposition, in any form, offers opportunities for undertaking investigations that become most familiar with creative writing practices. By doing so this develops experiential and procedural knowledge that is not otherwise accessible to critical analysis, using methods of testing that knowledge, and theories about practice, and developing hypotheses about how different approaches, techniques, imaginative conjectures and thoughtful engagements with ideas work in creative writing.

METHODS

Investigating creative writing can happen through the practice of creative writing and through the critical examination of actions and materials produced by a creative writer (you and/or others). Most often, and most productively, it involves a combination of both approaches. Most productively because such a combination mirrors the approach taken in creative writing, therefore harnessing the power of a conceptual metaphor. It provides the bedrock for informed reflection and, as creative writing involves action, it often results in your active response, most empowering your creative writing, sometimes propelling other forms of writing where discoveries are critically examined.

It is important to note that creative writing is being viewed here as a practice with many outcomes, not all of which are material outcomes. Additionally, that the reasons for someone doing some creative writing can be many and the value of both the doing of it and of the outcomes of it can be valued in different ways. It is true that for the most part we have tended to value creative writing according to an assessment of its 'literary' outcomes and to look mostly toward the cultural and commercial value of those end products. It is not that we have ignored the other values in and around the practice – such things as its display of human creativity, its links to strong standards of literacy, and its role in supporting self-expression, with its attendant positive psychological and social effects – but it is to the material end products we have largely turned when considering results and valuing those outcomes. Because creative exposition seeks to explore the *practice* of creative writing as well as the many *results* of creative writing the intention of its methods can relate to a wider range of activities and certainly a wider range of results.

Methods in creative exposition can therefore include (these are often entwined or connected, work in partnership or work in association):

- **'Practice-led research'** or **'research through practice'** or **'practice-based research'** – the combination of creative practice and critical examination of that practice, influences on it, ways it occurs, themes and subjects associated with it, techniques, aesthetics, explorations that are genre-based, or connected to societal influences or observations, psychological considerations, philosophic investigations, and more.

- **Textual analysis** – taking into account that creative writing indeed involves writing (that is, inscribing) and that this writing produces texts and that those texts (of many kinds, and not all complete) offer the opportunity for our consideration and interpretation. Textual analysis can be primarily about content or context, about language, about the 'micro' elements of a text or texts (words, sentences, rhetorical techniques) or the 'macro' elements of a text or texts (the discourse of an entire work or of many works connected by subject or theme or historical time) or about the role of a text or texts in the interactions between people. It can be a combination of these approaches.
- **Action-based and observational approaches** – individual or group, whereby creative writers or a creative writer (yourself, others) conduct investigations by identifying research questions, and then approaching them from a number of angles (sometimes called 'triangulation') whereby the actions are undertaken, participated in and/or observed, what is found is reflected upon and interventions, changes, addresses to particular problems are suggested.
- **Quantitative research** – this is not very common in creative exposition, given that it suggests, at least casually, the idea of the quantification of creativity or the measurement of the imagination – notions that might of course be impossible, and that at the very least are not widely well-received. That said, examples could include the

consideration of readerships or audiences in terms of how works are received (numbers of readers, numbers of hits on a game or a song or a digital poem), or the analysis of the frequency of the appearance of certain tropes, or characters or types of description). Quantitative research might apply more to some genres than others, and be linked to wider considerations of the impact of works of creative writing in the creative industries; or it might be used to gauge involvement in types of creative writing education, thus reflecting on how creative writers are formally learning, or to be used to count structural aspects of rhythm or the comparative length of chapters or be applied to assessing the range of works published on a particular topic or at a particular time.

- **Specifically narrative, situational or cultural analyses** – creative exposition in which the story of a work or works are told, perhaps the biographical or autobiographical exploration of how the creation of a work relates to a period in the creative writer's life or the cultural background, the national or local context, or the particular events of a particular piece of history, or the grounded aspects of a particular habitat, its cycles of days, seasons, the year, its natural or made environment, or the examination of the relationship between the creative writer's individual story and the story of others, family, those from the same background or place.

- **Reader/audience response approaches** – here an examination of how readers/audiences react or reacted to completed works, drafts, work presented privately or publicly. For some creative writers this might be an investigation not unlike professional market research, whereby works are substantially formed, and your creativity informed, by the reactions of readers or audiences who are polled along the way to a work's completion. For other creative writers the investigations here are about informing personal judgments in the light of external opinion – and this might be the responses of a very few, well-known respondents (family, friends) or the responses of an anonymous mass (for example, responding to the online posting of a work-in-progress). The investigation here might concern reactions that are sought out or a consideration of reactions to previous work in light of new work you're undertaking. In some instances, a creative writer might intentionally not seek out reader/audience responses and make an element of their critical understanding their thoughts on how they imagined and incorporated into their work their idea of their reader, an imaginary guide that could perhaps define a relationship built on envisioned empathy.

LEARNING AND TEACHING CREATIVE WRITING

That creative practice is not without critical understanding is self-evident in that we know all creative practitioners incorporate knowledge and understanding into practices, and in doing often explore ideas, observations and emotions in ways that contribute both to their personal understanding and to the understanding of those who engage with their work or works. We know also that writing is schematic and is a form of communication and a form too where the originator is not necessarily in the room with the receiver. So writing inscribes, records, gives longevity to ideas, thoughts, emotions, observations, provides for transportability of these and offers opportunities for exchange between human beings over time and place that could not otherwise happen. However, it is also reliant on intellectual engagement that makes the communication it offers exchangeable, especially when further informed by our individual imaginations. Commonsensically then, it has to be built on forms of shared understanding and knowledge. In spite of all this, in education we have often formally separated critical analysis from creative practice, differentiating intellectual work from imaginative work, and often formalizing this in the ways in which we have constructed educational programs and particularly courses. Creative exposition, in its acknowledgement of both the imagination and the intellect, and in its exploration of actions and evidence found in many modes, at a variety of times and in a range of forms, gives us the tools we need to investigate creative writing both for our own purposes as creative writers and generally to contribute to the storehouse of human knowledge.

Your creative exposition benefits from you establishing aims, objectives and projected outcomes. Those outcomes can be singular or many, can be purely practical or broadly intellectual, they can be creatively exploratory or specifically related to a situational issue that is preventing your progressing a project or that you feel is in some way limiting your creative writing overall. Aims (what you are going to do) established, objectives (why you are going to do it) considered and outcomes (what will be achieved, created, determined) projected, you have a choice of methods (ways of investigating) available to you, and the decision on which methods to choose, when and to what ends, will be determined by an often iterative process of returning to your needs, your curiosity, your sense of progress, your desire to know more, your confronting of situations in your creative writing and perhaps even by the responses of others to the work you do and the work or works you send out into the world.

As a way of informing learning, creative exposition clearly also has a role in the teaching of creative writing and, I'd suggest, has long been found in the classrooms and workshops of those teaching creative writing, even if it has not been labeled as creative exposition. While undoubtedly as an approach it is eclectic, multi-faceted and often highly individualized, the potential truths unearthed through creative exposition make it invaluable in creative writing pedagogy and, though not previously brought together as a conceptual and constructive term, brings together critical approaches to creative writing that have long been identified and have been frequently employed.

Included in your development of your own creative exposition therefore can be as many areas of interest and exploration and investigation as there are approaches, subjects and themes in creative writing. Considering your aims, objectives and projected outcomes, your focus might be on the physical labor of creative writing, on aspects of meaning and literacy displayed, on the symbolic, on the encoded nature of the language used, or on the observable patterns in your work or the work of other creative writers. You could consider the cause and effect aspects of your imaginative conjectures, or their connective nature or your use of fact in these creative journeys. What you prioritize, how you perceive things, people, events – this too could be a focus. Your navigation of time and place, how you draw on the local, the global, what ways your creative writing uses time structures, or how you approach the combining of the writing activities of foundation, generation and response. All this also is potentially part of your creative exposition. Your individual motivation, beliefs and identity.

Creative exposition can be methodologically holistic, drawing on the societal, cultural, political, economic influences around you, perhaps making comparative assessments, based on how your creative writing occurs in your world of today and others in worlds of previous years or in other parts of the globe very different from your own. So holistically grounded considerations, whereby large entities (such as nations, culture, people in general) are considered in relation to creative writing or your undertaking of creative writing. Alternatively, creative exposition can be methodologically individualist, concentrating on your individual practices, identity, psychologies, the micro and macro elements of your compositional choices, how your own skills, knowledge, beliefs, feelings are involved in your creative writing, influence it, can be explored through it and in it. In both holistic and individualist instances the reminder that creative writing is a form of communication is never far away, as the majority of creative writers will at some point exchange the results of their efforts with someone else, one individual, or an entire globe of individuals.

Your creative exposition can explore the models you use in your own work or the models used by other creative writers. It can work through narrative or comparative analysis, consideration of text or technique or exploration of audience response. Within your creative exposition you can employ observation, consider emotional contexts, your personal interests, core ideals, and thoughts, and research structures, forms, concepts and meanings – in your creative writing, and/or in the creative writing of others. Often creative exposition will work through synapses, or the sparking of connections between one element of your practice and another, or between the outcome and how you consider that outcome or between your imagination and your intellect. These synapses will create a union that is represented by the work you do and the works you produce. In other words, the network of activities, those synaptic sparks, the propelling forward of your projects – these things are collaboratively linked and form the basis of a complete picture of your creative writing.

The evidence you draw upon in order to explore what you do, how you do it, why you do it, and what results from you doing it, is considerable, varied and diverse. The value attributed to elements of this evidence might not always be culturally or economically universal and in order to do creative exposition well it might be necessary for you confirm how that evidence has been influential and in what ways it tells a story of creative writing or informs a particular critical opinion. Your analytical tools might be descriptive, qualitative, causal and inferential. On many occasions they may be predictive – not simply as an intellectual exercise in wondering what might occur in your creative writing or in the creative writing of others, but specifically attempting to predict what the results of an element of your practice might be, how you might improve an approach, or introduce a new technique, or draw upon an alternate range of influences, or incorporate new feelings or attempt to master a previously unused style, or engage with a genre, or appeal to a different audience, or complete a work that you have for some time struggled to complete but that you feel must ultimately be done to express something you wish to express in creative writing and through your pursuit of creative writing. The possibilities for creative exposition are considerable, and as an approach for critically approaching creative writing, it provides the tools and the means for improving your knowledge and for developing and ultimately applying your understanding.

REFERENCE

For a discussion of situational knowledge in creative writing see:

Harper, G. (2013) Creative writing research. In *A Companion to Creative Writing*, 1st ed. Oxford: Wiley-Blackwell, 284.

CRITICAL APPROACHES TO CREATIVE WRITING

What follows is a short creative exposition checklist, posed as questions. This is not intended to be a complete list of questions, it is merely to provide you with a mnemonic aid, establishing some signposting as you further establish, develop and explore your critical approaches to creative writing. Creative writing involves synapses, the sparking of connections, communication between the creative and the intellectual, between thinking, feeling and acting, between the imagination and the inscribing. If you are a creative writer, as this book largely assumes you are, then how you critically approach creative writing will often depend on what situations you face in your creative writing. Such situational knowledge – that is, the pursuit of knowledge that can assist you in progressing your writing, solve a problem you're facing, or contribute to your understanding of a current and sometimes future writing need – such knowledge is applied knowledge, born out of need and borne forward on the assumption of future use of the discoveries you make. But creative exposition also involves developing knowledge that is broadly experiential (that is, relating to the experiences of creative writing) and procedural (that is, relating to the courses of action available to you) and theoretical (that is, concerned with general principles and propositions) and your creative exposition might seek to contribute to these avenues of knowledge as well.

Critical approaches to creative writing, the creative exposition you employ to display and explain, for yourself and/or for others, combines individualist and holistic methods, the former connected with personal actions and results and the latter situating actions and results in broadly cultural, social, economic, and political conditions. Together, supported by the idea that creative writing is a distinctive form of human endeavor that is complex but accessible to us. Such methods involve determining your particular critical goals at any given time (for example, you seek to determine structure in a poem, or you aim to solve a problem with characterization, or you want to create a different prose rhythm or you're trying to determine the voice of your screenplay). Guiding you in your critical approaches can be a set of questions or statements or hypotheses that focus how you approach your analysis and when you determine that you have succeeded (or, indeed, failed in some instances) to add to your store of knowledge and improve your understanding. Mnemonics in the form of questions can be mapped in the first instance onto the areas explored here in *Critical Approaches to Creative Writing*; from there the simplest guide will always be what it is that you are trying to achieve.

For some creative writers it might be that your creative exposition is mostly connected with seeking satisfaction for your self-expression. For others it might be what you are seeking is commercial success for a particular creative writing work you have in mind. For others still, it might be that you want to convey to an audience a certain feeling, a valuable experience or a particular thought or thoughts about an event, about something in society, about how some activity in the world might be viewed. There is no single definition of satisfaction connected with creative writing that must take precedence over another definition. Creative writers seek to 'bring something into being' for a variety of reasons. While it is true that writing involves learned technical skills, which can be more or less developed in any one creative writer, and that creativity can be highly individualized, stronger or weaker in any one person, the satisfaction any of us gains from our creative writing is ultimately connected with our goals for that creative writing and with our expectations of success or failure related to those goals. Critical approaches to creative writing best begin by defining what it is you seek to achieve and why you seek to achieve it. From there, your creative exposition is determined by the critical goals you set yourself, what you seek to discover, the actions involved in your creative writing and the outcomes (material and nonmaterial) of your creative writing. Some of the outcomes will be along the way to a final iteration of a work or works of creative writing. Some might happen without any final material work ever being produced. Some will be directly connected to a final iteration of a work, and their existence might indeed be vested in that work. Some outcomes will be core to the practices you undertake. Some will be an outgrowth or byproduct of those practices. Questions to assist you in setting your critical investigations in motion could include some of these:

CHAPTER ONE: WRITING WITH IMAGINATION

- How is your creative writing being inscribed? In what way, via what device or devices and to what degree of likely permanency?
- The physical labor of writing creatively – can you determine the patterns of this and how the physicality of the practices is managed?

- What symbolic dimensions does your creative writing explore? Are these all on the same plane of reference or do you use the figurative and literal in a way to support each other across planes of reference?
- What codes does your creative writing carry – such things as the marking of particular occupations, cultural conditions and backgrounds, social position, age? Writing is encoded and creative writing, empowered by the imagination, has the potential to be encoded by a considerable range of references?
- What observable patterns does your writing present, graphic, and/or also in terms of word choice and employment, patterns of expression and phrasing, explanation, description?
- Does your imagination seem to work to produce factual, memory explorations, counterfactual explorations or fantastical explorations? Do you in fact combine these?
- What appears to be your imagination's schema or schemas – the combining or contrasting or speculating – that you creatively initiate and pursue?
- How do your imaginative conjectures, the journeys you go on in your creative writing (the particular project you're working on, or generally) related to sensory information you receive, to the work of your intellect?
- What role does salience play in how you use your imagination in creative writing? What determines what is relevant for you to include in your work, the directions that work takes, the things, events, people, circumstances you imagine but choose to leave out?
- What aspects of observation, feeling or consideration does your imagination combine? In other words, do you take from one experience, add something from another experience, bring together things from the past and the now?

CHAPTER TWO: CREATIVE WRITING INFLUENCES

- If listing the most prominent influences on your creative writing (for an individual project or in general) what would you include? How do these influences manifest themselves in your practices and your outcomes?

- Creative writing takes time. How do you manage to do it? Does availability of time influence what you do, the genre you write, the topics you gravitate toward, your pursuit of opportunities to see the results of your creative writing published or performed?

- Temporal shifts in creative writing can be employed in many ways. In what ways do you employ time in your creative writing and to what ends?

- Are the results of your creative writing 'timely'? Do you ever consider what you are writing in terms of the penchant of contemporary readers or audiences and, if so, how does this influence your creative writing?

- If your work is set somewhere – as often works of creative writing are – is that setting both a situation in time as well as a situation in place?

- Where do you write? Does this directly relate to how you write, what you write, and for whom you write – or all of these and perhaps more?

- What are your 'research materials' for your creative writing? Are people an element of those research materials? Is so, whom?

- Is the condition of the local, regional, national or international arena an influence on your creative writing in a discernible way? Do you seek this out or simply know it is the case?

- What motivates you to write creatively? What do you believe in that influences your creative writing? Who are you, and

113 Checklist

how do you relate to others around you? Do others influence your creative writing in certain ways – whether those 'others' are people you know well, people you meet or fantastical entities you invent from the characteristics of people you've observed or imaginatively projected into being?

- What is the knowledge you employ, explore and/or seek in your creative writing?
- What models (if any) do you use to guide your compositional practices, the shape of your working and ultimately the shape of any final works that emerge? Do you favor visual models, figurative models based on nature or on some other guiding principle?

CHAPTER THREE: CREATIVE WRITING PRACTICES

- A broad consideration of your writing practices yields you what information? That is, do you detect something about how you form the idea for a work, or develop that idea, or refine that idea? Are you largely focused on an 'end' that is some time and distance away or are you shaping your creative writing based on accumulating elements (episodes, observations) without any sense of how this accumulation might become a firmly shaped thing?
- What in your creative writing (the project you're working on or generally) happens first, what happens next? Do some things more often happen simultaneously?
- Can you define your foundational practices?
- How do your generational practices differ from those foundational ones? How long does it most often take to move from action that establishes to a project to a position where you feel you are generating it, moving it along?
- If generational writing involves both creating and recreating what judgments do you make to determine when

something needs to be 'recreated'? How do you confirm the validity of your judgment?

- Taking your creative writing and responding to it, do you seek out other opinions than your own? If so, who to do you seek out, why, and to what ends?

- Creative writing involves synapses – points at which transfers occur between your imagination and your intellect, energy is generated around a feeling or an idea or an observation or a thought, things are connected and often communication ultimately initiated between you and others. Around what do these synapses occur in your creative writing?

CHAPTER FOUR: EXPLORING CREATIVE WRITING EVIDENCE

- Treating your creative writing for one moment as if it is a library or a museum or live performance in which you are immersed, what kinds of evidence can you find?

- Material and nonmaterial evidence is available to us – can you create a typology of evidence in and about your creative writing that is reflective of both these conditions?

- What evidence relates to why you create and what relates to how? In what ways are these connected?

- Can you determine the evidence available to you that provides you with the most information about your creative writing? What is it?

- The evidence you find has played a role in some way – but the roles played might well be vastly different, depending on the evidence you're examining. What roles have been played, when, and to what effect?

- Taking evidence of your creative writing (or, if you like, that of someone else) can you compare this evidence with that produced by another creative writer, or a group, or across time and place, or in a different genre? What does comparative analysis of the evidence of creative writing reveal to you?

- You've determined that there is both material and nonmaterial evidence and considered the varieties of these. What sources have you used to explore these? How trustworthy are these sources? For example, you have a library of favorite books going back several years, how do you determine which if any offer evidence of influence on your stylistic, thematic or subject choices, and how do you validate that determination?

- When analyzing evidence are you mostly describing what it is, how it has been part of your creative writing practice, and what has resulted from it being part of your creative writing practice? Alternatively, or additionally, are you looking for textual examples of influence, attitude, approach, thought, feeling?

- Do you use both qualitative and quantitative analysis when considering evidence of creative writing?

- Are you looking for a narrative of cause and effect; that is, the story of how something influenced an action and what action or actions were influenced?

- Does evidence of creative writing (yours, others) offer some predictive capabilities? For example, can you determine through examination of evidence that if you create one character, a personality of a certain kind, in a short story you will inevitably almost always create another character, a personality of another kind, as a foil for that character? Does the evidence you examine suggest you prefer to compose to a certain rhythm or adopt a certain point of view – and in predicting this does examination of that evidence give you the tools to better develop your pacing, your use of tense?

CHAPTER FIVE: DEVELOPING CREATIVE EXPOSITION

- Why do you want to critically approach creative writing, solely for the benefit of your own creative writing, and primarily to apply what you discover? Alternatively, both to make discoveries related to your own work and contribute to a wider pool of knowledge. Solely to contribute to a wider pool of knowledge, with no plans to use the information to inform any creative writing of your own?
- Are the reasons for your creative exposition connected with solving a compositional problem, more generally with progressing a project, attempting to create models that you can use for the next section of your project, for your next project or for any foreseeable future project?
- What methods are you using for your critical investigations – practice-led research, action-based research, textual analyses, reader/audience response analysis, a combination of these or other methods?
- How would you define your aims (what you are doing) and objectives (why you are doing it) of your creative exposition?
- In summary, what are the projected outcomes of your creative exposition, what do you expect to accomplish and to what ends?

Creative writing involves a structured and ordered use of a shared and commonly understood language and the inscribing of that language into written words. It is distinctive from other kinds of writing in that the original, the new and the inventive are heightened. Creative writing is also distinctive in that we aim specifically to create, to 'bring into being', through the purposeful use of written language and the application and employment of our imaginations. To critically approach creative writing involves considering its practices and outcomes from the point of view of the imaginative and of the intellectual, and its nature from the point of view of the creating, as well as from the point of view of what is ultimately created. By doing this as creative writers we increase our personal knowledge of our creative writing practices with pragmatic and potentially lifelong results. By doing this generally we contribute to a pool of human knowledge about a practice and a variety of artistic and communicative outcomes that have long been admired, are often celebrated and are frequently acknowledged for contributing to the lives we lead.

Index

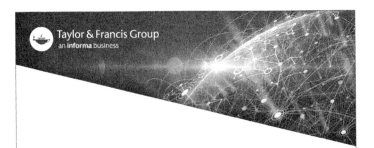

Printed in Great Britain
by Amazon

76561163R00088